SPELLING
it out

RHIANNEDD PRATLEY

D0348245

BBC BOOKS

Published to accompany a series of programmes, prepared in consultation with the BBC Continuing Education Advisory Council

This book is published in conjunction with the BBC television series *Spelling It Out*, first transmitted on BBC1 from October 1988. The series was produced by Charles Pascoe.

Cartoons: Roger Fereday

Acknowledgements

pages 97 and 99: *The Pocket Oxford Dictionary* (Oxford University Press, 1984)
page 100: (top) *Black's Writing Dictionary* (A & C Black, 1972); (centre) *Collins Pocket English Dictionary* (Collins, 1981); (bottom) *Harrap's Pocket English Dictionary* (Harrap, 1983)
page 114: *Androcles and the Lion: with a parallel text in Shaw's Alphabet* (Penguin, 1962)

Published by BBC Books
A division of BBC Enterprises Ltd
Woodlands, 80 Wood Lane,
London W12 0TT

First published 1988
Reprinted 1988 (three times) and 1989 (twice)

© The authors 1988

ISBN 0 563 21437 6

Typeset in 10/12 Plantin by Ace Filmsetting Ltd, Frome, Somerset
Printed and bound in Great Britain by Richard Clay Ltd, Bungay, Suffolk
Cover printed by
Richard Clay Ltd, Norwich, Norfolk

FOREWORD

I am an editor of dictionaries. I spend all my working time thinking about words: how they have been formed, what they mean, how they are pronounced, and how they are spelt (or spelled!). I receive a lot of feedback from users of dictionaries too. It is clear to me from all this information and thought that what worries people most in the ordinary use of English from day to day is spelling. We can usually cope with not knowing what a particular word means or how it is pronounced, because it is likely to be a more complicated word that we meet less often and can avoid saying. But spelling difficulties affect the simplest of words that we need to write all the time, such as *its* and *there*, as well as the long complicated words we only use occasionally. The written word is so important in our everyday lives that it is difficult to imagine language without it, and clear and accurate writing depends very heavily on good spelling.

Spelling It Out is an excellent book because it adopts the standpoint of the user of English. It shows the user how to break words down into manageable elements and how to explore ways in which words are related to one another. I have added a section (pp. 104–114) that shows how knowing about the history of English can help us understand why it seems more difficult to spell than other languages. I have also tried to explain why and how far English – more than most languages – allows alternative spellings like *inquire* and *enquire*, and to explain the part dictionaries play in all this and why one dictionary can differ from another.

There are many claims made about English that I find very questionable. I do not believe that English is a 'bigger' language (in terms of the number of words) than others, nor that English has more words for the same thing than others (*stone*, *pebble*, etc.); there is simply not enough evidence for making such comparisons. In any case, I do not think they are the real point. It is all too easy to be chauvinistic about one's own language, but I do believe that what makes English exceptional among the languages of the world is that it is firmly in the hands of its users; that it can absorb influences and develop and adapt itself in a remarkable way; and that its 'rules' are no more than a report on the present state of the language as received by us, its users, from our predecessors.

I think this book understands and builds very well on these features, and will greatly help all those who use it; to them I extend my very best wishes in improving their spelling.

Robert Allen
Editor,
Concise Oxford Dictionary

CONTENTS

INTRODUCTION

Does spelling matter?

If you're reading this book, spelling probably matters to you. You may think it matters to the people who will have to read what you write. You're probably correct on both counts. Spelling does matter. Whether it *should* matter is another question. People often judge us by the way we write, which seems rather unfair when you think about the difficulties presented by the English spelling system.

Very few people master the system completely. Most of us manage quite happily with the words we use regularly until we need a less familiar word. Then the problems arise. But even then mistakes don't matter as long as the writing is 'for our eyes only' – or perhaps for the immediate family.

It's when our writing is read by other people that spelling really begins to matter.

Why does spelling matter?

When we read we should be able to ignore the spelling and cut straight through to what the writer is saying. Unfortunately, we can only do this when the spelling is correct. Spelling mistakes draw attention to themselves and catch the eye, distracting the reader from the main task of getting the writer's message. At worst they can be so bad that they make it difficult to understand what the writer is saying. At best they irritate the reader and cause him or her to think that the writer is careless or incompetent. Either way the reader probably won't give the sort of attention the writer would wish. A piece of writing can't do its job if the reader is paying attention to the spelling and not to what the writer is saying.

'I can't be doing with this lot. Throw out all the ones with messy writing or spelling mistakes. Just leave me the ones that are easy to read.'

Poor spellers aren't usually careless. They tend to take great pains to get the words right and this means that all too often they think in ten-letter words but write in three-letter words that they can spell! People simplify their writing to avoid seeming incompetent, sometimes to a point where it no longer represents the quality of their thinking. Those who want to take full control of their lives and influence other people need the tools for making good writing. One of these tools is good spelling.

Will this book teach me to spell?

No. This book can't deal with YOUR particular spelling problems. They are personal to you. We're all different and we make different mistakes. To improve your spelling you must look carefully at the words YOU spell wrongly, decide what you need to learn, find a way of remembering, and practise the words you're trying to master.

That's what YOU have to do. What will the book do?

- Show you techniques of learning which will make your memory for spellings more effective.
- Show you that many words fall into 'spelling groups' and that you can develop a system for dealing with them.
- Give you information about the English language and encourage you to develop an interest in words. You will need this if you are going to be a good speller.

Think about this

No one can teach you to spell. But people can show you what to learn and how to learn it.

How to use this book

The aim of this book is to show you how to extend the range of words you spell confidently, and how to tackle words that you don't regularly use. You can use it in several different ways. You probably won't want to start at the beginning and work your way all the way through to the end. No two people have exactly the same spelling difficulties, so the book is designed for you to 'dip in and out' as you wish.

This is a small book. It covers *most* kinds of spelling problem, but it does not claim to include absolutely every technique, rule or exception. For people who want to take things further, there is a Booklist on page 128.

Words like 'noun', 'verb' and 'adjective' are used from time to time and these are all explained in the Glossary on page 117.

There is a section on using dictionaries, starting on page 97. For people who don't possess one, some alternatives are suggested in 'Ten Tips for getting by' on page 101. If you're thinking of buying a dictionary, shop around until you find one that suits you. There are plenty about. And if you're wondering how to look up a word if you can't spell it, there are some helpful hints in the section 'Listening to word beginnings' starting on page 38.

Finally, people only need to spell if they're going to write. So this is a book for *writing in*. Once you've learned how to spell a word, the only way to fix it in your memory is to write it several times until you get used to the feel of it. So please read this book with a pen or pencil in your hand!

DEALING WITH SINGLE WORDS

If your spelling is not too bad and you only need help in tackling the odd word here and there, this part of the book will help you:

A1   Memory aids - mnemonics This section will show you how to develop your own ways of learning and remembering how to spell the words you find particularly difficult.

A2   Using syllables This section will show you how to tackle words you haven't spelled before. It's particularly useful for longer words.

A3   Look/say/cover/write/check This section explains an effective technique for remembering whole words. It uses all the senses involved in spelling.

A4   Homophones This section will help you with words which sound the same as other words but have different spellings.

A1

MEMORY AIDS – MNEMONICS

A self-help approach to single words

Most people could reel off a list of words they always spell wrongly. Yet, with a little effort, these could be mastered. A useful approach is to invent a memory aid for the problem word. These memory aids are called MNEMONICS (pronounced 'nemonics' – the 'm' is silent). This section will help you to devise your own mnemonics to fit your personal problem words. This involves:

● comparing your misspelling with the correct word and working out where you're going wrong;
● inventing a mnemonic (a way of remembering) for the part you get wrong;
● practising the correct form of the word.

Did you know?

The word mnemonic comes from the Greek word 'mnemon' which means 'mindful'.

How do mnemonics work?

Take the word necessary. It's often spelled wrongly. The error is usually in the number of 'c's and 's's.

1 Find the right spelling, in a dictionary perhaps, and *compare* it with your version.

necessary

neccessary x

necesary x

2 Ask yourself why you spelled it wrongly.
- Did you have the letters in the wrong order?
- Did you leave out letters?
- What exactly went wrong?

no

yes

I'm confused about which letters, if any, are doubled.

3 Ask yourself what you need to remember about the word in order to spell it correctly.

I need to remember there's one c but double s

4 Write the word correctly and underline the parts you need to concentrate on.

ne<u>c</u>e<u>ss</u>ary

5 Invent a mnemonic to help you with this specific problem.

Example of mnemonic
It is necessary to have one collar (one 'c') and two socks (double 's').

6 Fix the spelling in your mind with the

LOOK/SAY/COVER/WRITE/CHECK

method described on page 21.

14

The success of the method lies in the amount of mental processing which takes place. It doesn't matter how silly the mnemonic is. It's the process of inventing it that's important. By the time you've made it up you'll probably have remembered the spelling.

Other people's mnemonics may not help you but here are some ideas to think about.

■ Alter the pronunciation so that you emphasize the spelling patterns.

Wed – nes – day	Wednesday	main – ten – ance	maintenance
pe – ople	people	mort – gage	mortgage
marri – age	marriage	fri – end	friend

■ Find a hidden word and highlight it.

You must **add** your **add**ress.

A **secret**ary keeps a **secret**.

Never se**para**te a **para** from his **para**chute.

SE/PARA\TE

I am sitting in parl**iam**ent.

A **govern**ment must **govern**.

There's **sin** in bu**sin**ess.

An island **is land** surrounded by water.

IS\LAND

■   When words have very unusual letter combinations and you are thoroughly confused, invent a sentence using the letters in the right order.

Rhythm – **R**hythm **h**as **y**our **t**wo **h**ips **m**oving.

Phlegm – **P**eople's **h**ealthy **l**ungs **e**xpel **g**ood **m**ucus.

Try making your own sentence mnemonic. Use the letters of **diarrhoea** – a word which often needs to go on a sick note! Practise the spelling below.

diarrhoea
diarr....

d –
i –
a –
r –
r –
h –
o –
e –
a –

Think about this

The mnemonics we remember best are the silly or vulgar ones!

A2

USING SYLLABLES

Cutting long words down to size

Have you had the experience of wanting to use a really interesting word and finding that you just can't sort out the spelling? It's at times like that when you go for the easy short word and your writing 'sells you short'. In this section we shall look at a way of dealing with longer words. This strategy is called SYLLABIFICATION. It involves dividing words into SYLLABLES.

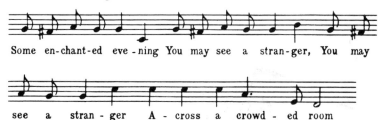

How to hear the syllables

A syllable is the smallest part of a word which can be spoken separately.

Say these words:

| remember | liar | across |
| picture | opportunity | experience |

Each word can be said in such a way that the separate syllables can be heard.

re-mem-ber (3 syllables)	li-ar (2 syllables)
pic-ture (2 syllables)	op-por-tun-it-y (5 syllables)
a-cross (2 syllables)	ex-pe-ri-ence (4 syllables)

17

If you are not sure how to break a word into syllables, try singing it. You will need one note for each syllable:

♪ ♪ ♪ ♪
a–pol–o–gize

♪ ♪
sing–le

♪ ♪ ♪
de–cid–ed

♪ ♪ ♪ ♪ ♪ ♪
syl–lab–if–ic a–tion

If you can't sing, tap your fingers.

Some words have just one syllable each: God save the Queen.

How to recognize a syllable

- A syllable will always contain at least one vowel or the letter 'y' which can act like a vowel:
  us–u–al–ly; sen–ti–men–tal.

- A syllable could be a vowel on its own:
  um–brell–a; tom–a–to; a–pol–o–gize.

- A syllable may contain two vowels next to each other which make one sound:
  con–tain; sta–tion.

- A syllable will never be a consonant on its own.

Did you know?

Out of the 26 letters in the alphabet,
- **5 are vowels: 'a' 'e' 'i' 'o' 'u';**
- **'y' is sometimes a vowel and sometimes a consonant;**
- **the rest are consonants: 'b', 'c', 'd', 'f', etc.**

Why is it useful to know about syllables?

When you break a word into syllables you can tackle one small part at a time. The spelling task becomes more manageable. If you make a mistake you can quickly see which part of the word you need to concentrate on.

Say **experience** and break it into syllables.

    ex-pe-ri-ence

You now have four small pieces to work on.

ex   Many words start with this as a syllable:
          *ex*it; *ex*tend; *ex*cellent; *ex*ceptions.

pe/ri   Both these syllables have a similar sound 'EE' (in stan-
          dard pronunciation) but use different letters. By working
          on syllables you will become used to different ways of
          spelling the same sound.

ence   This is a syllable which occurs at the end of many words:
          confer**ence**; excell**ence**; audi**ence**; conveni**ence**;
          resid**ence**; influ**ence**.

Now try the examples below and on the next page.

Say the words below then break them into syllables. Say each syllable as you write it. The first two have been done for you. Add some examples of your own.

WORD	SYLLABLES	NUMBER OF SYLLABLES
experience	ex pe ri ence	4
audience	au di ence	3
convenience	_____	4
sentence	_____	2
beginning	_____	3
admitting	_____	3
apartment	_____	3

WORD	SYLLABLES	NUMBER OF SYLLABLES
across	_____	2
application	_____	4
faithfully	_____	3
detect	_____	2
protect	_____	2
congratulations	_____	5
maintenance	_____	3
immediately	_____	5
Sincerely	_____	_____
acknowledge	_____	_____

Some people like to write out a word on a strip of paper, cut it up into syllables, shuffle the pieces and then reassemble them.

LOOK/SAY/COVER/WRITE/CHECK

Whichever technique you use for *learning* the spelling of a word, the next thing is to train yourself to *remember* it. The best way of doing this is to *picture the whole word* in your mind's eye and *practise it by writing it in one go*, without looking back at the original. The technique is called LOOK/SAY/COVER/WRITE/CHECK.

Here's what you do:
Pick a word you want to learn and write it clearly, making sure it's spelt correctly before you start.

Example   **acknowledge**
MAKE SURE IT'S SPELLED CORRECTLY BEFORE YOU START LEARNING IT!

1   **Look** at it carefully. Don't just glance. *Study* it.
2   **Say it**. There are three syllables: ac/know/ledge. *Notice* the beginning, middle, end in the right order as you say it. Try to get a *picture* of the whole word in your mind.
3   **Cover** the word you have learned.
4   **Write** the word in one go without looking back at the original. *Don't look back to check letter by letter*. If you get stuck, cross it out. Look back at the original and try again.
5   When you've finished, and not before, look back at the original and **check** if you're right.

Practise this technique on words of your choice in the space below.

Word   Word

_____   _____

_____   _____

Points to remember about LOOK/SAY/COVER/WRITE/CHECK:
- DON'T COPY LETTER BY LETTER. If you do you are spoiling your chance of learning the visual picture of the whole word.
- When you've 'got' a word, PRACTISE IT!
- When you are revising a word you've learned some time ago, look at the correct spelling before testing yourself. This will refresh your visual memory. It's not cheating – it's a better way to learn.

Did you know?

We have about 44 sounds in the English language and only 26 letters to make them with. That is why many letters have more than one sound, and often letters combine to make a different sound.

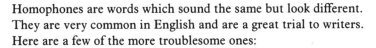

A4

HOMOPHONES

Homophones are words which sound the same but look different.
They are very common in English and are a great trial to writers.
Here are a few of the more troublesome ones:

to	too	two	whose	who's
there	their	they're	your	you're
its	it's		here	hear

The mistakes made with homophones are not really spelling errors,
they are *meaning* errors. The word you use may be spelled correctly
but it might be the wrong word for the meaning you want to put
over.

Homophones are confusing *because* they sound alike. If you want
to be able to tell the difference between them you must try to ignore
their sound and find other ways of learning them.

What is the best way to learn homophones?

If you are confused over words which sound alike, deal with them
separately. Trying to learn them together will make you even more
confused. Choose one of the homophones and master it before trying to learn the others. The individual words can be learned either
through their meanings or their 'look'.

1 Learn them through their meanings

When you're writing you know what you want to say but you can't
always spell the words you need to use. When the word you need
has a homophone – a counterpart which sounds the same – it's even
more difficult. You have to produce the right string of letters for

23

the word which means what you want to say. If you produce the wrong string of letters they will mean something entirely different. A *bare*-faced liar might not be a very nice person, but a *bear*-faced liar would worry you even more!

'And the one that got away was this tall!'

When you are learning a homophone think about its meaning. There's a lot of difference between a tuba and a tuber! Learn it together with words which have a similar meaning.

Learn these separately

here (at this place)	hear (to hear sounds)
hereby	hearing
hereabouts	heard
hereafter	hearsay (gossip, rumour)
herein	unheard of
herewith	overheard

You will find that by concentrating on the meaning, in time you will automatically choose the spelling pattern which gives you the word for what you *mean*.

2 Learn them by their 'look'

When two words can be confused by their sound (whose, who's) it's important to memorize the distinctive visual appearance of each one. When you are deciding which word you need, you must be able to form in your mind a strong visual image of the word which gives the right meaning. To do this you need to link the word with others which have the same pattern of letters.

Example
Who's
> The man who's standing there is the one who's parked his car in the director's space.
> (who's=who is or who has)

The apostrophe (') is used here to show that letters have been missed out. It is the distinctive part of this word. Learn it with other words that also have **'s**:

who**'s** – who is/has   she**'s** – she is/has
he**'s** – he is/has   it**'s** – it is/has

Whose
1 Whose car is parked in the director's space?
2 The man whose car is parked in the director's space will have to move.
(whose=who does it belong to?)
-ose is the important letter pattern. Learn it with other -ose words:
> whose   chose   those

'I'm a dead loss at spelling but you should hear me play the homophone!'

Some common problems

1 Their/They're/There

In this passage the three homophones are used correctly. Read through the passage and think about what the three different words mean. When you have decided which one you need to work on, go on to the page which deals with that word.

'See that train over *there* on Platform 4?' the	line 1
porter said to the ticket collector. '*There* are two	line 2
blokes in a first-class compartment and *they're*	line 3
travelling on second-class tickets. *Their* cases are	line 4
in the end carriage, but *there's* standing room	line 5
only down *there*.'	line 6
'I know them,' said the ticket collector. '*They're*	line 7
there every night on that 6 o'clock train. Every-	line 8
one knows what *they're* up to, but the guard never	line 9
catches them at it. *They're* going to sit *there* until	line 10
they see the guard at the end of the carriage, then	line 11
they're off to the buffet car, so they don't have to	line 12
pay the excess on *their* tickets.'	line 13
'*They're* going to get *their* money's worth out of	line 14
British Rail,' said the porter.	line 15
'Not tonight, *they're* not,' chuckled the ticket	line 16
collector. '*There* are two guards on that train, one	line 17
at each end, and *there's* no buffet car!'	line 18

This passage is reproduced on page 30 with the homophones left out. When you're sure you can use them all correctly, fill in the blanks.

Their

Their always means *belonging to them*:

    line 4 – *their* cases (the cases belonging to them);
    line 13 – *their* tickets (the tickets belonging to them);
    line 14 – *their* money's worth (the money belonging to them).

Their is a *possessive* word. You use it when you want to say that something is owned by more than one person or thing.

Their is the *plural* of his, her, its.

Put these sentences into the plural. The first one is done for you.

The *man* picked up *his* wages at the office.

The *men* picked up   *their wages at the office*

When is the *car* going for *its* MOT?

When are the *cars* going for   _____

Did the *nurse* get *her* pay rise?

Did the *nurses* get   _____

The *horse* was led by *its* trainer into the paddock.

The *horses* were led by   _____

They're
They're always means *they are*. Re-read the passage opposite but say **they are** every time you see **they're**.

The apostrophe between **they** and **re** shows that the **a** of **are** has been dropped. **They're** is the *short form* of **they are**.

Finish off these sentences with your own ideas.

They are going to increase   _____

_____

My wife and daughter will not be coming because they are

_____

I'm afraid they are much too   _____

_____

Don't believe a word they say. They are   _____

_____

Now rewrite the sentences on the next page using *they're* instead of *they are*.

_____

_____

_____

_____

_____

_____

_____

_____

Learn *they're* with other short forms:
   they're = they are
   you're = you are
   we're   = we are

Substitute the short form for the words in italics below, and
then read it through in a natural way.

Jack and I are going to the bowls club social with the Wilsons.
They are taking their car and *we are* having a lift with them.
I'm sure *you are* welcome to come with us if *you are* willing to
squeeze in the back.

_____

_____

_____

_____

There

There can be used in two ways:

- To show a place. It tells you *where* something is happening.
- In sayings like 'there is', 'there are', etc.

There – meaning a place

These examples are from the lines of the passage on page 26:

    line 1 – that train over *there*
    line 6 – standing room only down *there*
    line 8 – *there* every night
    line 10 – they're going to sit *there*

To help you remember *there* as a *place* word, learn it with other *place* words which have the same letter pattern:

    there – thereabouts; thereby; thereto
    here   – hereabouts; hereby
    where – somewhere; nowhere; anywhere

Practise writing this sentence in the space below

Where is it, here or there?

There is, there are, etc:

These examples are from the lines of the passage on page 26:

    line 2 – *there are* two blokes
    line 5 – *there's* standing room only (there's=*there is*)
    line 17 – *there are* two guards on that train
    line 18 – *there's* no buffet car (there's=*there is*)

Try this way of using 'there' by completing these sentences in your own way. Practise them in the space below.

Today there is   _____

_____

Tonight there are   _____

_____

Tomorrow there will be   _____

_____

Fill in the blanks in the passage below when you are confident you have learned how to use *their*, *they're* and *there* correctly. Re-read the passage on page 26 before starting. Think about the *meaning* of the words which are missing.

'See that train over _____ on Platform 4?' the porter
said to the ticket collector. '_____ are two blokes in a
first-class compartment and _____ travelling on sec-
ond-class tickets. _____ cases are in the end carriage,
but _____ standing room only down _____.'
  'I know them,' said the ticket collector. ' _____
_____ every night on that 6 o'clock train. Everyone
knows what _____ up to, but the guard never catches
them at it. _____ going to sit _____ until
they see the guard at the end of the carriage, then _____
off to the buffet car, so they don't have to pay the excess on
_____ tickets.'
  '_____ going to get _____ money's worth
out of British Rail,' said the porter.
  'Not tonight, _____ not,' chuckled the ticket collector. '_____ are two guards on that train, one at each
end, and _____ no buffet car!'

---

2 Two/Too/To

In this passage the three homophones are used correctly. Read the passage and think about what the three different words mean. When you have decided which one you need to work on, go on to the page which deals with that word.

The *two* women paused *to* peer through the win-	line 1
dow of the shop. It was really *too* early *to* stop for	line 2
afternoon tea but their attention had been caught	line 3
by a trolley laden with cakes which were *too*	line 4
tempting *to* resist.	line 5
They were supposed *to* be at the cathedral by	line 6
ten *to* four, *to* meet the rest of their group, but the	line 7
thought of another hour walking around a dusty	line 8
old church was *too* much *to* bear. Mary turned	line 9
to her friend, 'Tea for *two*, Kath?'	line 10

> 'Sounds great *to* me,' said Kath. 'We can go *to* the cathedral tomorrow.'
> The shop was empty except for *two* schoolboys who looked up guiltily when the door opened, as if they, *too*, should be somewhere else.
> 'What are you going *to* have, Kath? I'm going *to* go mad and have a chocolate éclair.'
> 'Me *too*!' said Kath. 'I might even have *two*! If we're going *to* the devil we might as well go happily!'

| | |
| line 11 |
| line 12 |
| line 13 |
| line 14 |
| line 15 |
| line 16 |
| line 17 |
| line 18 |
| line 19 |
| line 20 |

This passage is reproduced on page 33 with the homophones left out. When you're confident you can use them all correctly, fill in the blanks.

Two

Two means 2. It is always used as a number:
   line   1 – the *two* women
   line 10 – tea for *two*
   line 13 – *two* schoolboys
   line 18 – I might even have *two* (éclairs)

Two contains the letter 'w'. This makes it look different from its two (2) homophones (to/too).

Learn it together with other numbers:
   2 – **tw**o
   12 – **tw**elve (two + ten)
   20 – **tw**enty (two × ten)

Learn it with other words which have a similar meaning:
   two   – 2
   twins   – two children
   twice   – two times
   be**tw**een – between two things

Too

We use *too* in 2 ways:
● to mean 'excessively', e.g. too late; too cold.
● to mean 'also' or 'as well'.

These examples are from the lines of the passage on pages 30–1:
  line 2 – it was really *too* early (excessively early)
  line 4 – *too* tempting
  line 9 – *too* much
  line 15 – they, *too*, should be somewhere else (they, as well as the women, should be somewhere else)
  line 18 – me *too*! (me, also!)

If you can substitute 'also' or 'as well', the word you need is '*too*'.

Substitute 'too' for the words in italic.

Like my father, I *also* am a writer. He wrote novels and travel books. So do I, but I write poetry *as well*.

_____

_____

_____

Complete these sayings. They all contain 'too'.

Example   Too close for comfort.

  _____ _____ _____ spoil the broth.

  _____ _____ for his boots.

  It's never _____   _____ to learn.

Apart from 'too', the words you'll need are:
  late; big; many cooks

To

Use *to* as part of a verb when you want to say 'to do something'.

line 1 – *to* peer	line 7 – *to* meet
line 2 – *to* stop	line 9 – *to* bear
line 5 – *to* resist	line 16 – *to* have
line 6 – *to* be	line 17 – *to* go mad

Use *to* before a noun or pronoun to show 'going towards'.
line 7 – ten *to* four   line 12 – *to* the cathedral
line 10 – *to* her friend   line 19 – *to* the devil
line 11 – *to* me

Note: 'To' is the most common of these three homophones. It is also the most difficult to explain. The easiest approach is to learn the meaning of 'two' and 'too', then 'to' will fall into place.

When you are writing, concentrate on the meaning you want to express. If you mean a number 2, use *two*. If you mean 'also' or 'as well' or if you want the homophone to mean 'excessively', use *too*.

Fill in the blanks in the passage below when you're confident you have learned how to use *two*, *too* and *to* correctly. Re-read the passage on pages 30–1 before starting. Think about the meaning of the missing words.

The _____ women paused _____ peer through the window of the shop. It was really _____ early _____ stop for afternoon tea but their attention had been caught by a trolley laden with cakes which were _____ tempting _____ resist.

They were supposed _____ be at the cathedral by ten _____ four, _____ meet the rest of their group, but the thought of another hour walking around a dusty old church was _____ much _____ bear. Mary turned _____ her friend, 'Tea for _____, Kath?'

'Sounds great _____ me,' said Kath. 'We can go _____ the cathedral tomorrow.'

The shop was empty except for _____ schoolboys who looked up guiltily when the door opened, as if they, _____, should be somewhere else.

'What are you going _____ have, Kath? I'm going _____ go mad and have a chocolate éclair.'

'Me _____!' said Kath. 'I might even have _____! If we're going _____ the devil we might as well go happily!'

---

3 Its/It's

In this passage the two homophones are used correctly. Read the passage and think about what the two different words mean. When you have decided which one you need to work on, go on to the page which deals with that word.

It's a fact that most people get mixed up between	line 1
its and *it's* and yet *it's* an easy problem to	line 2
solve. What's surprising is that *it's* been a problem	line 3
to many people who ought to know better. I've	line 4
seen the wrong one used on a British Rail poster,	line 5
on an order form from a book club, and in a report	line 6
from an Education Department.	line 7
British Rail should choose *its* poster writers	line 8
more carefully; the book club should reprogram *its*	line 9
word processor, and the Education Department	line 10
should put *its* own house in order before telling	line 11
anyone else how to teach.	line 12

This passage is reproduced opposite with *its* and *it's* left out. When you're sure you can use these words correctly, fill in the blanks.

Its

Its without an apostrophe (') is a possessive word.
Its means *belonging to it*:
    line 8 – British Rail should choose *its* poster writers . . .
    line 9 – the book club should reprogram *its* word processor, . . .
    line 11 – the Education Department should put *its* own house . . .

Learn *its* together with other *possessive* words.
We went to the races and:
    I lost *my* purse
    You lost *your* shirt
    He lost *his* self control
    She lost *her* dignity
    The horse lost *its* rider
    We lost *our* way
    They lost *their* winnings.
The words in italics are all possessive words.

Write sentences about:

- Spelling and its problems
- British Rail and its sandwiches
- The BBC and its programmes
- The TUC and its members

It's
It's with an apostrophe always means *it is* or *it has.*

Read through the passage opposite and see where you can substitute *it is* or *it has.*
You can use *it is* in lines 1 and 2.
You can use *it has* in line 3.
You cannot use *it is* or *it has* in lines 8, 9 and 11.

When writing, decide if you can use 'it is' or 'it has'. If you can, then it's safe to use *it's* with an apostrophe.

Fill in the blanks in the passage below when you're confident that you have learned how to use *its* and *it's* correctly. Re-read the passage opposite before starting. Think about the meaning of the missing words.

_____ a fact that most people get mixed up between its and it's and yet _____ an easy problem to solve. What's surprising is that _____ been a problem to many people who ought to know better. I've seen the wrong one used on a British Rail poster, on an order form from a book club, and in a report from an Education Department.

British Rail should choose _____ poster writers more carefully; the book club should reprogram _____ word processor, and the Education Department should put _____ own house in order before telling anyone else how to teach.

CRACKING THE SYSTEM – TACKLING GROUPS OF WORDS

So far we've looked at ways of learning single words. But we can't learn every word separately. We must find some means of cracking the system. In this part of the book we'll be looking at ways of tackling *groups* of words.

Good spellers attack words from several directions; if one approach fails they try something else. Poor spellers often don't know a variety of approaches. They may even be hooked on one approach.

If you can master some of these approaches, or even be aware of them, you will be able to attack unknown spellings more confidently and have a better chance of being right. These are the approaches we shall be looking at in Part B:

B1 Sounding it out The sound of a word is very often *not* a satisfactory guide to its spelling. But it can *sometimes* be useful to listen to the beginnings and ends of words.

B2 Some useful rules Most English spelling rules are complicated and there are always exceptions. This section looks at just a few rules which can help with common spelling errors.

B3 Prefixes and suffixes These are the 'bits' which are added to the beginnings and ends of words to make new families of words linked by their meanings.

B4 Using the meanings of words Many spelling mistakes can be avoided by thinking about the meaning of a word instead of its sound.

B1

SOUNDING IT OUT

'Sounding it out' is the method most widely used by poor spellers when they're trying to spell a word they don't know. For many people it's the *only* method they know. They can get 'hooked' on it, not knowing what else to try. Unfortunately sounding out doesn't always work because there's no *reliable connection* between the way we prounounce words and the way we spell them.

It may work for some words.

It may work for parts of many words.

BUT you can't rely on the sound to give you the spelling of the majority of words you need for everyday use.

You may have been taught to believe that words are *supposed* to be spelled the way they sound. You may even think that if the sound and the spelling don't match, it's because you're not speaking 'properly'. That's nonsense! You may be able to match some words with your speech but there are many more spellings which will never match their sound, however carefully you pronounce them.

e.g. Wednesday; said; was; any; many.

And what about the words which sound the same but are spelled differently?

e.g. to, too, two;

      right, write, rite, wright.

You can't tell the difference between these spellings by listening to the way you say them.

However, the sound of a word will always give you some clues to its spelling. In particular it can be useful to listen to the beginnings and ends of words. The difficulty is that there are often many ways of writing the same sound. But if you combine the use of sounds with the other spelling methods in this book, you will improve your chances of getting words right.

Listening to word beginnings

1 Single beginning sounds

Probably the most reliable part of a word to listen to is the beginning. If you can tell what the first letter is, you can at least find the word in a dictionary.

But beware, even at the start of a word there may be alternative ways of writing the sound.

Below is a list showing the alternative ways of writing some initial (beginning) sounds. Add your own words to the appropriate column, checking each one in a dictionary.

If you can't think of any words starting with the more unusual letters like 'gn', 'ph', 'sc', find some in a dictionary and pick those which would be most useful to you.

Sound			
'c' (cat)	catch *collar*	kettle *kitchen*	chemist *Christmas*
	___	___	___
	___	___	___

Sound		
'f' (fat)	forward *finish*	photograph *physical*
	___	___
	___	___

Sound		
'g' (girl)	garden *gear*	ghost *ghetto*
	___	___
	___	___

Sound 'j' (jam)	just *jockey* ——— ———	generous *ginger* ——— ———	
Sound 'n' (not)	necessary *neither* ——— ——— pneumonia ——— ———	knife *knot* ——— ———	gnome *gnash* ——— ———
Sound 'r' (run)	remember *risk* ——— ———	rheumatism *rhyme* ——— ———	
Sound 's' (sit)	settee *sandwich* ——— ———	cigarette *century* ——— ———	scissors *scent* ——— ———

Sound 's' (sit)	psychology		
	_____		
	_____		

Sound 't' (ten)	temper tack	Thames	pterodactyl
	_____	_____	_____
	_____	_____	_____

Sound 'w' (water)	Wednesday work	what white
	_____	_____
	_____	_____

2 Blended beginning sounds

When words start with more than one consonant, the first consonant seems to slide into and blend with the next one.

start play snap twist scratch

It's difficult to hear the letters separately when you sound out the
word, but if you can recognize them as 'blends' of letters it will give
you a good chunk of the word to start off with.

If you make lists of words which contain the same initial blends
of letters, you may find you are able to hear them more clearly.
This will help you recognize those combinations of letters at the
start of words whose spelling is unknown to you.

On the next pages are examples of words starting with the most
common consonant blends. Add to these lists by using a dictionary

and choosing words which would be useful to you. Read the lists aloud so that you see, hear and 'feel' each word. (You'll feel what you're doing with your tongue and lips as you say the letter blend.)

Add your own words to this list using a dictionary.

bl	br	cl	cr
black	bring	climb	crane
blinker	bread	clown	create
___	___	___	___
___	___	___	___

dr	dw	fl	fr
dry	dwell	fly	friend
dreadful	dwindle	flour	french
___	___	___	___
___	___	___	___

gl	gr	pl	pr
glance	grown	plaster	proud
glove	grey	pluck	prince
___	___	___	___
___	___	___	___

sc	scr	sl	sp
scar	scratch	sly	spend
scotch	scrounger	slide	speech
___	___	___	___
___	___	___	___

spl	spr	shr	squ
splash	spray	shred	squeeze
splendid	spring	Shropshire	squirrel
___	___	___	___
___	___	___	___

st	str
steel	stretch
stop	strangle
___	___
___	___

tr	thr	tw
trip	three	twin
tread	thread	twitch
___	___	___
___	___	___

Think about this

Millions of people have learned to spell regardless of how they talk. If you want to be a better speller, think about words in other ways than just their sounds.

Take the letters below and add them to the end of consonant blends shown in the previous exercise.
You will be able to use some of the blends more than once.

-ay   bray; clay _____

_____

-and   bland; _____

_____

-ee   flee; _____

_____

-oud   cloud; _____

_____

-one   _____

_____

-ash   _____

_____

-arf   _____

_____

-y   _____

_____

-inkle _____

_____

Warning This exercise shows why it's dangerous to rely on the sound *only*: eg 'Pl' + 'and' sounds like a proper word (planned) but the spelling is wrong. Use your dictionary to check each word.

Listening to word endings

The end of a word is often very difficult to hear. In natural speech we tend to run one word into the next or to drop the end of a word completely:

A hot dog salesman dropped dead after a health inspector
found dead bats in his meat mincer.

This is another reason why the sound of a word may not be much of a guide to its spelling.

Sometimes you can hear the last syllable clearly enough for it to be useful in the spelling:

clear**ly**	*clearly*	pro**tect**	*protect*
gradual**ly**	_____	re**ject**	_____
separate**ly**	_____	se**lect**	_____
love**ly**	_____	con**nect**	_____
faithful**ly**	_____	de**tect**	_____

By making lists of words which have the same endings you'll gradually become aware of the patterns you're likely to come across.

One reliable sound to listen out for is the sound at the end of pi**ck** and pan**ic**. It's the same sound spelled two ways.

–ick		*–ic*	
sick	*sick*	picnic	*picnic*
pick	_____	attic	_____
trick	_____	traffic	_____
thick	_____	automatic	_____
stick	_____	fantastic	_____

Notice that when the sound comes at the end of a short word with one syllable it is spelled –ick. If the sound comes at the end of a word with more than one syllable it is spelled –ic. Apart from one or two names (e.g. Vic, Patrick) there are no common exceptions.

Using –ick as your ending, write a list of one-syllable words starting with the following consonants or consonant blends: e.g. lick; stick.

k; l; p; qu; r; s; t; w; br; cl; cr; fl; pr; sl; st; tr.

kick _____

_____

_____

Did you know?

Many of the longer words ending in –ic were once spelled –ick – 'magick', for example, and 'tragick'. Now we only get –ick in these words when we add –ing, –er, –ed; e.g. panicky, picnicker, drug trafficking.

Read these words, noticing the syllables and the –ic ending.

atomic	metric	Atlantic	classic
comic	horrific	Pacific	critic
topic	plastic	Arctic	domestic
magic	electric	mechanic	scientific
logic	arithmetic	music	terrific
picnic	traffic	tonic	scenic

Use some of these words to fill in the blanks below:

Jimmy Tarbuck is a stand-up _____

+ − ×: These are all symbols used in _____

A meal out of doors is a _____

The sort of shock you get if you touch a live wire: _____

Metres and litres are _____ measurements.

Name two oceans: _____ _____

A _____ spell

A pick-me-up: _____

He'll fix your car: _____

Clear thinking: _____

Anything to do with the home: _____

Anything to do with science: _____

B2

SOME USEFUL RULES

The good news is, there *are* some rules about English spelling. The bad news is, they are very complicated to explain and there are always exceptions.

Even good spellers, who must be following the rules, are not always aware of the rules they are using. They have learned the rules by doing lots of writing. Eventually they acquire a feeling for how words are likely to behave. They are following rules without realizing it.

These words are following a rule. Write them out in the spaces provided. Work down the columns.

excellent	decide	legacy
excellent	_____	_____
ice	acid	bicycle
_____	_____	_____
receive	cigarette	juicy
_____	_____	_____
accent	science	cyst
_____	_____	_____
central	circle	cyclone
_____	_____	_____
sincerely	city	vacancy
_____	_____	_____

Compare the sound of the 'c' in the words above with those below.

de**c**ay	**c**oncrete	a**c**ute
decay		
re**c**all	be**c**ome	res**c**ue
ea**ch**	pra**c**tise	**c**ry
a**ch**e	a**c**tor	se**c**ret
in**c**lude	pi**c**nic	so**ck**
class	a**c**ne	te**ch**nique

To discover the rule:
- listen to the sound made by **c** in each word
- look at the letter following the **c**

Rule (fill in the boxes)

When **c** is followed by the letter ☐, ☐ or ☐ it sounds like **s**.

Test the rule by scanning through the word list on pages 122–8.
The **c** will sound like **S** every time it's followed by **e**, **i** or **y**.

In this section we'll look at those rules which could help with some of the more common spelling errors.

But first a word of warning!
Don't spend time learning the rules. Practise the words which are examples of the rule. This way you'll get the feel of how these words behave and you'll be able to work out the rule, even if you can't put it into words. Where possible spaces have been left for you to write in the examples after you have looked at them.

1   The 'i' before 'e' rule

When you ask people if they know any spelling rules this is usually the only one they can remember.

'i' before 'e' except after 'c'.

But this is only half the rule.

> If you want to make the sound **E** – it's **i** before **e** except after **c**.
> If you want to make the sound **A** or **I** – it's **e** before **i**.

The lists below show this rule in action. To practise the rule:
- read through the list of examples (work down the columns);
- look at each word in turn and write it in the space provided, saying it as you write.

To make the sound E

i before **e**   except after **c**

chief *chief*   believe _____   receive _____

brief _____   reprieve _____   receipt _____

grief _____   relieve _____   perceive _____

grieve _____   relief _____   deceive _____

field _____   niece _____   deceit _____

yield _____   piece _____   conceive _____

diesel _____   achieve _____   conceited _____

shield _____   siege _____   ceiling _____

shriek _____   pierce _____

priest _____   fierce _____

Exceptions: seize, weir, weird, protein, and various names such as Sheila, Neil, Keith. Also sheikh, either and neither if you pronounce them with an E sound.

---

*To make the sound A or I – **e** before **i***

a sound		**i** sound
eight	vein (for blood)	height
eight		
eighty	rein (for a horse)	either
eighteen	reign (of a queen)	neither
weight	neigh (of a horse)	eiderdown
sleigh	skein (of wool)	
veil	neighbour	

Some other **ei** words are leisure, forfeit, foreign.

2   Plurals of nouns ending in 'f' or 'fe'

(Nouns are words which are the names of things.)
● Usually just add **s**
chief *chiefs*   cliff *cliffs*

safe _____   tariff _____

*roof _____   *handkerchief _____

*It's a common error to change the **f** to **ves** in these words, but this is not correct.

- Sometimes change **f** to **v** and add **es**

wife *wives*   shelf *shelves*

life _____   self _____

knife _____   elf _____

thief _____   leaf _____

loaf _____   calf _____

wolf _____   half _____

- Sometimes you have a choice
scarfs or scarves   hoofs or hooves
turfs or turves   wharfs or wharves

3   Plurals of words ending in 'o'

- Most just add **s**,
especially if they are
   words introduced fairly recently from other languages: kimonos, banjos, sombreros;

kimonos _____

   musical words: solos, sopranos, concertos, oratorios;

_____

   words ending in two vowels: zoos, tattoos, studios, cameos, cuckoos.

_____

- Some add **es**
Many of these are common, everyday words:

potato *potatoes* _____   torpedo _____

tomato _____   domino _____

cargo _____   tornado _____

volcano _____   buffalo _____

echo _____   mosquito _____

4 Very few English words end in 'i', 'u' or 'v'

There will nearly always be a silent **e** after these letters

give _give_	glue _____	pie _____
have _____	rescue _____	die _____
solve _____	blue _____	lie _____
receive _____	true _____	tie _____

Exceptions: these tend to be abbreviations, slang or words introduced fairly recently from other languages: e.g. taxi, mini, ski, emu, guru, Peru, div, spiv.

Did you know?

'Derv' stands for diesel-engined road vehicle.

5 Very few English words end in 'j'

The J sound at the end of a word will be made by the letters **ge** or **dge**.

edge _edge_	garage _____	huge _____
ridge _____	marriage _____	siege _____
badge _____	college _____	sausage _____

Exception: Raj.

6   *When you add 'all' to the beginning of a word, use one 'l'*

all + though	although	*although*
all + so	also	
all + most	almost	
all + ready	already	
all + one	alone	
all + ways	always	
all + together	altogether	

Exception: all + right stays as two words: *all right*.
'Alright' does appear in the dictionary but many people do not consider it to be correct.

7   *When you add 'full' to the end of a word, use one 'l'*

- Usually add –ful to the base word with no change:

help + ful = helpful *helpful*

hope + ful = hopeful _____

spoon + ful = spoonful _____

play + ful = playful _____

forget + ful = forgetful _____

use   + ful = useful _____

- Sometimes you have to change the end of the base word (for an explanation of 'base word' see page 55).

If the base word ends in a consonant + **y**, change the **y** into **i**:

beauty + ful = beautiful _____

fancy + ful = fanciful _____

If the base word ends in **ll**, drop one **l**:

skill + ful = skilful _____   will + ful = wilful _____

Did you know?

Most dictionaries give the correct plural of 'spoonful' as 'spoonfuls', though some regard 'spoonsful' as an old-fashioned alternative. The same applies to other words ending in '-ful'.

Add –ful to the words below, taking care to change the ends of the base words marked *.

wonder _wonderful_   *beauty _beautiful_

thought _____   *plenty _____

success _____   *pity _____

hand _____   *mercy _____

joy _____   *fancy _____

faith _____   *will _____

force _____   *skill _____

use _____   mouth _____

hate _____   eye _____

hope _____   care _____

cup _____   sin _____

Two other important words to learn:
awful (the base word is awe but the **e** is dropped) _____
grateful (grate comes from the Latin word 'gratus' meaning 'thankful') _____

Note When you add **-ly** to a word ending in **-ful**, the double **l** is included.

beautiful +ly=beautifully _____

grateful   +ly=gratefully _____

thankful +ly=thankfully _____

merciful +ly=mercifully _____

hopeful   +ly=hopefully _____

useful   +ly=usefully _____

skilful   +ly=skilfully _____

wilful   +ly=wilfully _____

successful+ly=successfully _____

awful   +ly=awfully _____

PREFIXES AND SUFFIXES

Prefixes and suffixes are the 'bits' which are added to the beginnings and ends of base (or root) words to make new words. This gives rise to a family of words linked by their meaning.

Forgiveness, unforgivable, misgivings, given – this is a family of words built up from the base word 'give' by adding different prefixes and suffixes:

Prefixes	Base word	Suffixes	New word
	give		
	giv(e)	en	given
	giv(e)	ing	giving
for	give		forgive
for	give	ness	forgiveness
un|for	giv(e)	able	unforgivable
mis	giv(e)	ing|s	misgivings

Sometimes the end of the base word changes when you add an ending (suffix). In the example above the silent 'e' is dropped before adding –en; –ing; –able.

In some words, letters are doubled or changed before suffixes. In this section we shall look at the rules which will help you recognize where the changes will occur.

> **Warning** This is a long and difficult section. Don't try to take in too much in one go. Take a bit at a time, practise the examples and add your own examples where you can.
>
> It will be worth making the effort because if you know about prefixes and suffixes you can be more logical in your approach to spelling. You will also have a better understanding of the English language.

Prefixes

Prefixes are put in front of a base word. These are some of the most useful:

ante- (meaning=before) antenatal; anteroom; antecedent
anti- (meaning=against or opposite to) antibiotic; anticlimax; antifreeze
auto- (meaning=self) autograph; automatic; autobiography
dis- (meaning=not or away) disappear; dissatisfied; dishonest
*ex- (meaning=out of) expel; export; exclude
in- (meaning=not), sometimes written as *il-, im-, ir-* invisible; illegal; immoral; irregular
inter- (meaning=between) international; interrupt; interrogate
mis- (meaning=wrong) mistake; misconduct; misspell
pre- (meaning=before) precede; prefix; present
pro- (meaning=for or forward) progress; protest; proceed
re- (meaning=again or back) remind; remember; return; remake
sub- (meaning=under) suburb; submission; substitute
super- (meaning=above) supervisor; superior; superman
trans- (meaning=across) transport; transatlantic; transfer
un- (meaning=not or in reverse) unavailable; unnatural; unusual

* When 'ex' is used to mean 'former', the word is always hyphenated, e.g. ex-wife, ex-colleague.

Building words by adding prefixes

There are two things to remember about prefixes:
1 If the last letter of the prefix is the same as the first letter of the base word, there will be a double letter.

Prefix dis-
dis+satisfied =dissatisfied *dissatisfied*
dis+solve =dissolve _____
dis+sent =dissent _____

but
dis+embark =disembark _____
dis+play =display _____
dis+rupt =disrupt _____

Prefix un-

un+natural   =**unn**atural _____
un+necessary =**unn**ecessary _____
un+nerving   =**unn**erving _____

but

un+usual   =**un**usual _____
un+happy   =**un**happy _____
un+easy   =**un**easy _____

2 Sometimes the prefix will change to match the first letter of the base word. This will give a double letter.

Prefix in-

in- is sometimes written as il-; im-; ir-, depending on the first letter of the base word.
il- before words starting with **l**
ir- before words starting with **r**
im- before words starting with **m**, but also before **b** and **p**

il- before 'l'
il+legal _____
il+legitimate _____
Exceptions: inlay, inland

ir- before 'r'
ir+regular _____
ir+reproachable _____
Exception: inroad

im- before 'm'
im+moral _____
im+movable _____
Exceptions: inmate, inmost

im- before 'b'
im+balance _____
im+bibe _____
Exception: inborn, inbred

im- before 'p'
im+proper _____
im+polite _____
Exception: input

in- before 'n'
in+numerable _____
in+nocent _____
Exception: ignoble

in- before all other letters
in+different _____
in+correct _____
in+appropriate _____
in+excusable _____

Make the negative forms of the words below by adding the prefixes given to the base words. Check all your answers with the word list on page 122.

Add in-, im-, il-, ir- or ig-

proper	*improper*	rational	_____
moral	_____	mediate	_____
legible	_____	press	_____
decent	_____	legal	_____
audible	_____	competent	_____
mobile	_____	resistible	_____
prove	_____	human	_____
possible	_____	migrant	_____
responsible	_____	reversible	_____
logical	_____	numerate	_____
balance	_____	mature	_____
noble	_____	replaceable	_____

Add un- or mis-

carriage	*miscarriage*	even	_____
take	_____	shapen	_____
natural	_____	necessary	_____
lead	_____	spent	_____
popular	_____	conduct	_____
usual	_____	aided	_____

Add re- or dis- (some words will take either)

honour	*dishonour*	construct	_____
open	_____	satisfied	_____
usable	_____	act	_____
able	_____	comfort	_____
armament	_____	ease	_____
grace	_____	arrange	_____
entry	_____	service	_____

Suffixes

Suffixes are put *after* base words. Here are some of the more common ones. It is helpful to separate them into those starting with a vowel and those with a consonant.

Vowel suffixes

–able/–ible
audible; capable

–al
medical; regal

–ar; –er; –or; –eer
vicar, farmer, actor, mountaineer

–ation/–ition
conversation; partition

–ed
recorded; jumped

–en
sadden; happen

–er, –est
bigger; biggest

–ing
dancing; carrying

–ity
scarcity; locality

–ize/–ise
advertise; criticize

–ous
nervous; courageous

–y
noisy; thirsty

Consonant suffixes

–ful
wonderful; beautiful; spoonful

–less
careless; useless

–ly
sadly; happily; poorly

–ment
judgement; argument

–ness
happiness; fitness

Did you know?

With many words there is a choice between –ize and –ise, e.g. criticise, criticize. Some people prefer –ize, which is closer to the Greek –izo from which this ending has developed and we have used –ize in this book. It is common in American usage. Unfortunately there are some words which *must* be spelled –ise because their origin is not the Greek –izo but something else. For example, 'televise' comes from the Latin 'vis' meaning 'see'. This is why many people prefer to use –ise all the time as it is never wrong.

Building words by adding suffixes

Sometimes the base word changes when you add an ending (suffix). It depends whether the suffix starts with a vowel or a consonant.

We shall look at four different groups of words and see how they behave when suffixes are added to them.

Group 1   Words ending in silent 'e'

Examples
  hope   use   gentle   believe
  safe   bare   notice   manage

When you add a consonant suffix – no change
  hopeful hopeful   useless _____   gentleness _____
  safety _____   barely _____   management _____

Exceptions: argue + ment = argument _____
true + ly = truly _____
judgment or judgement (optional) _____
awe + ful = awful _____

When you add a vowel suffix – drop the 'e'

hope+ing=hoping *hoping*   believe+able=believable _____

use+ed   =used _____   notice+ing =noticing _____

noise+y =noisy _____   expense+ive =expensive _____

Exception: when you add the suffixes **ous** or **able** to some words ending in **ce** or **ge**, keep the **e**.

notice +able=noticeable *noticeable*

service +able=serviceable _____

change +able=changeable _____

manage +able=manageable _____

courage +ous=courageous _____

outrage +ous=outrageous _____

Also: age+ing=ageing *or* aging.

Build new words by adding suffixes to the words below.

Remember Drop the 'e' before a vowel suffix.

care (–ful; –less; –ing) *careful, careless*

caring

sincere (–ly; –ity) _____

improve (–ment; –ed) _____

laze (–y; –ing) _____

believe (–able; –er) _____

expense (–ive) _____

adventure (–ous; –er) _____

reverse (–ible; –al) _____

converse (–ation) _____

endure (–ance) _____

continued overleaf

B

Remember Some words ending in **ce** or **ge** keep the **e** before **-ous** and **-able**.

notice (-ed; -ing; -able) _noticed, noticing_

noticeable

service (-ed; -ing; -able) _____

_____

pronounce (-ed; -able; -ment) _____

_____

peace (-able; -ful) _____

gorge (-ous) _____

courage (-ous) _____

encourage (-ment; -ed; -ing) _____

_____

manage (-ment; -able; -ing; -ed) _____

_____

Group 2   Words ending in 'y'

You can divide these into two groups:

Words ending in vowel+y	*Words ending in consonant+y*	
donkey	company	fancy
buy	marry	clumsy
delay	hurry	twenty
repay	worry	busy
convey	deny	fly
deploy	reply	try
envoy	lady	family

Words ending in vowel+y. When you add any suffix – no change

donkeys _donkeys_	repayment _____	playful _____
delaying _____	conveyance _____	buyer _____

Exceptions: gay+ly=gaily *gaily* ____; day+ly=daily _____
lay+ed=laid _____; pay+ed=paid _____
say+ed=said _____

Words ending in consonant+y. When you add any suffix except **-ing**
– change the **y** *to* **i**

marry+age=marriage   deny+al=denial
busy+ness=business   rely+able=reliable
study+ous=studious   accompany+ment
twenty+eth=twentieth   =accompaniment

BUT

marry+ing=marrying   reply+ing=replying
fry+ing=frying   satisfy+ing=satisfying

Build new words by adding suffixes to the words below.

Remember If the word ends with consonant+**y**, change the
y to **i** before all suffixes except –**ing**.

lonely (–ness) _____

happy (–ly; –ness) _____

fly (–er; –ing) _____

bury (–al; –ing; –ed) _____

_____

heavy (–er; –est) _____

deploy (–ment; –ed) _____

employ (–ment; –ed; –er; –ee) _____

_____

carry (–ed; –age; –ing) _____

_____

marry (-ed; -age; -ing) _____

busy (-ness; -er; -est) _____

supply (-er; -es; -ed) _____

envy (-ous; -able; -ed) _____

It is useful to remember that to make the plural of words ending in consonant+'y', change the 'y' to 'i' and add 'es'.

Singular	Plural	Singular	Plural
supply	*supplies*	company	_____
lady	_____	sky	_____
factory	_____	spy	_____
dictionary	_____	ally	_____

Group 3 Words of one syllable ending with one vowel and one consonant

Examples

When you add a consonant suffix – no change

sin +ful =sinful _____   ship+ment=shipment _____
spot+less=spotless _____   sad +ly =sadly _____

When you add a vowel suffix – double the last letter

sin +er=sinner _____   ship+ing=shipping _____
spot+y =spotty _____   sad +er =sadder _____

Exceptions: words ending in **w** – row+ing=rowing

64

Build up new words by adding the suffixes in brackets to the words below.

Remember Double the last letter before a vowel suffix (-y is a vowel suffix).

skin (-less, -er, -y, -ful, -ed, -ing) *skinless, skinner, skinny, skinful, skinned, skinning*

glad (-ness, -ly, -en) _____

slip (-ing, -ed, -ery, -er) _____

man (-ful, -ly, -ish) _____

sin (-ful, -er, -ing) _____

sad (-ness, -ly, -er) _____

snob (-ish, -ery) _____

plan (-ed, -er, -ing) _____

fit (-er, -est, -ed, -ing, -ment) _____

wit (-y, -less, -ness) _____

beg (-ar, -ing, -ed) _____

cot (–age) _____

_____

rid (–ance) _____

_____

Group 4 Words of more than one syllable ending in one vowel and one consonant

Read these words aloud and notice where you put the stress or emphasis.

o**mit**	con**trol**	pre**fer**	be**gin**
re**gret**	en**rol**	con**fer**	for**bid**
com**mit**	pa**trol**	re**fer**	for**get**

The stress is on the last syllable. Compare them with these words:

target **mar**ket **bud**get **al**ter **lim**it

They have the stress on the first syllable.

Rule When the stress is on the last syllable of the base word, you double the last letter before adding a vowel suffix. There's no change when you add a consonant suffix.

Base word	Consonant suffix	Vowel suffix
com**mit**	commitment	committee *committee*
commit	*commitment*	committed _____
		committing _____
		committal _____
allot	allotment	allotted _____
_____	_____	allotting _____

Base word	Consonant suffix	Vowel suffix
forget	forgetful	forgetting _____
_____	_____	forgotten _____
		unforgettable _____
equip	equipment	equipped _____
_____	_____	equipping _____
enrol	enrolment	enrolling _____
_____	_____	enrolled _____
regret	regretful	regrettable _____
_____	_____	regretting _____
begin		beginner _____
_____		beginning _____

Exceptions
Prefer, **refer**, **confer** and **transfer** double their final letters for some vowel suffixes but not for others:
- preferred, preferring *but* preference, preferable
- referring, referral *but* reference
- conferred, conferring *but* conference
- transferred, transferring *but* transference, transferable

Rule If the stress is *not* on the last syllable of the base word, the final letter does not double unless it is an **l**.

Base word	Consonant suffix	Vowel suffix
target		targeted _____
		targeting _____
market		marketed _____
_____		marketing _____
budget		budgeted _____
_____		budgèting _____
alter		altering _____
_____		alteration _____
limit		limited _____
_____		limitation _____
offer	offertory	offering _____
_____	_____	offered _____

Special case – words of more than one syllable ending in one vowel and 'l'

These double the l before a vowel suffix, wherever the stress comes, unless the suffix is –**ity**, –**ise** or –**ize**.

Base word	Consonant suffix	Vowel suffix
travel		traveller; travelling
level		levelled; leveller
label		labelling; labelled
enrol	enrolment	enrolled; enrolling
annul	annulment	annulled
quarrel	quarrelsome	quarrelling
revel	revelry	revellers
cancel		cancelled; cancellation
equal	equally	equalled

Do not double the l before –**ity**, –**ise** or –**ize**

Base word	Vowel suffix
civil	civility; civilize
formal	formality; formalize
real	reality; realize
final	finality; finalize
legal	legality; legalize
equal	equality; equalize

Exceptions: tranquillity
            paralleled

Build new words by adding suffixes to the Group 4 words below. Find the correct answers in the word list.

Where the stress is on the last syllable of the base word, double the last letter before a *vowel* suffix, *except* where there is an asterisk *.

commit (ment; ee; ed) _____

_____

forbid (en; ing) _____

prefer (ed; ing; *ence; *able) _____

_____

regret (ful; s; able) _____

_____

Where the stress is not on the last syllable of the base word, do not double:

limit (ation; ed) _____

benefit (ed) _____

budget (ing; ed) _____

Where the base word ends in l, double the l before any *vowel* suffix except –ity and –ise/–ize.

label (ed; ing) _____

travel (er; ing) _____

enrol (ment; ed) _____

quarrel (some; ing) _____

equal (ed; ity) _____

real (ly; ize) _____

Summary of rules about adding suffixes

1 Words ending in silent 'e' (house, care)
Consonant suffix – no change (houseful, careless)
Vowel suffix – drop the 'e' (housing, cared)
(*See pages 60 and 61 for exceptions*)

2a Words ending in vowel+'y' (donkey, repay)
When you add any suffix – no change
(*See page 63 for exceptions*)

2b Words ending in consonant+'y' (busy, rely)
Before all suffixes *except* –ing, change 'y' to 'i'
busy – business, busiest *but* busying
rely – reliable, relied *but* relying

3 Words of one syllable ending in one vowel+one consonant (bat, slim)
Consonant suffix – no change (fatness, slimness)
Vowel suffix – double last letter (batter, slimming)
(*See page 64 for exceptions*)

4a Words of more than one syllable ending in one vowel+one consonant (other than 'l')
● If the stress is on the last syllable of the base word, double the last letter before adding vowel suffix:
commit   commitment (no change before a consonant suffix)
committee   committed   committal (double 't')
(*See page 67 for exceptions*)
● If the stress is not on the last syllable, the final letter does not double:
targeted; limited; offering

4b Words of more than one syllable ending in one vowel+'l'
Double the 'l' before all vowel suffixes, wherever the stress
(*except* before –ity, –ise and –ize)
traveller; patrolling; labelled; equalled
but equality; civilized/civilised; finality
(*See page 69 for exceptions*)

B

PREFIXES AND SUFFIXES

A word of comfort

If you feel thoroughly confused, remember this. The important thing is that, when you're trying to spell a long and difficult word, you *think* about whether parts of it are prefixes or suffixes. If you can recognize these bits, you can tackle the word in chunks, gradually building up the whole word.

If you can separate off the prefixes and suffixes, you have a better idea of the base word and can then think logically about whether to change its ending. You might not always be right, but you will know where you are making errors and will learn to cure these in time, with practice.

Think about this

Nobody remembers all these rules; most people don't even know they exist. Most of us pick out the words we *have* to write and bash away at these until we can tell when they *look* right.

B4

USING THE MEANINGS OF WORDS

Many spelling mistakes could be avoided by thinking about the meaning of a word instead of its sound.

When you're struggling with a spelling, instead of just listening to its sound to give you clues, try thinking of words to which it could be related. Words can be grouped together if they come from the same base or root and are linked together by their meanings, or if they have endings which give a particular meaning to a word. These words often contain the same letter patterns, and may look similar, even though they don't always sound the same.

Looking at the roots of words

Take the word SIGN.

It sounds like wine, dine, line, mine. However, we spell it **sign*** because it is related to words like **sign**al and **sign**ature. There are many words which have the –sign– letter pattern.

The following words are all related to 'sign' by their meaning. Note the –sign– letter string in each one.

sign	– a mark or indication *sign*
signal	– an indication that something will happen _____
signature	– your personal mark (your name) _____
signet ring	– a ring bearing a person's mark or seal _____
ensign	– the flag or mark of a military group _____
insignia	– badges or marks of rank _____
assign	– to mark out for a particular purpose _____

* The word 'sine' does exist as a technical term in trigonometry.

designer
designated
resignation
consignment
assignation

These words also belong to the 'sign' group but, because of the way we use them in modern English, their link with the word sign is not so clear.

'Sign' is a particularly useful word to illustrate the way words are linked by their meanings because there are so many words in its group. But even one related word might give you the clue you need to get a spelling right.

Did you know?

The word 'sign' comes from the Latin word 'signum' meaning mark or token.

Using related words to find the right vowel

In some words it's difficult to identify the vowel sounds, especially if they're not emphasized.

admiration   adoration   inflammation

When we say these words we tend to slip over the underlined vowels. The sound we hear is the same whether the letter is 'i', 'o' or 'a'.

If you can find words which come from the same root, in which the vowel is stressed, it will give you a clue to the spelling.

admiration   – admire (the 'i' is stressed)
adoration   – adore, adorable (the 'o' is stressed)
inflammation   – inflamed, inflammable (the 'a' is stressed)

On the next page there are more examples to practise.

Fill in the missing vowels in the words below. Try this with
the list on the right covered over. Then check your guess.
Practise the first word in the space on the right.

comb.nation	combine	_combination_
conserv.tive	conservation	_____
expl.ration	explore	_____
conf.rmation	confirm	_____
transf.rmation	transform	_____
persp.ration	perspire	_____
inf.rmation	inform	_____
re.l	reality	_____
decl.ration	declare	_____
sign.ture	signal	_____
gr.teful	gratitude	_____
libr.ry	librarian	_____
indigest.ble	digestive	_____
rel.tive	relation	_____
auth.r	authority	_____
defin.te	finite	_____
hypocr.sy	hypocrite	_____

USING THE MEANINGS OF WORDS

Using related words to find the right consonant

In some words consonants change or lose their sound when the word changes its ending.

medical – medicine

The 'c' changes its sound, but the spelling of that sound stays the same. In this way the words keep their visual similarity showing that they are related.

Here are more examples:

critic – criticize
signal – sign
damnation – damn
fact – factual ⎱ in practice, the 't' is usually pronounced like a 'ch'
act – actual ⎰ and this can be misleading.

Fill in the missing consonants in the words below. Try it with the right-hand list covered over. Then check your guess. Practise the first word in the space on the right.

sof.en	soft, softer	_soften_
len.th	long, longer	_length_
ac.ion	act, actor	_____
bom.	bombard, bombardier	_____
gra.ual	grade	_____
righ.eous	right	_____
an.ious	anxiety	_____
revi.ion	revise	_____
edi.ion	edit, editor	_____
contrac.ion	contract, tractor	_____
condem.	condemnation	_____
mali.n	malignant	_____

wi.th	wide, wider	_____
kno.ledge	know	_____
mus.le	muscular	_____
recei.t	reception	_____
phle.m	phlegmatic	_____

Fill in the blanks below with a word related to the one in brackets at the end of the sentence.

The sun was high and the cloudless sky offered no shade.

_____ ran down my neck and soaked my shirt.

(perspire)

The firm will accept a telephone order but will require

_____ in writing before dispatching the goods.

(confirm)

News of the hijack arrived too late to catch the early

_____ of the newspaper. (edit)

If you want to be sure of a seat, ring early and make a

_____ . (reserve)

Olympic swimming pools must be at least 50 metres in

_____ and 15 metres in _____ .

(long, wide)

Coca Cola. It's the _____ thing! (reality)

Your daily newspaper will give you _____ about

what's on television. (inform)

His test paper showed he was particularly weak in General

_____ and would need a lengthy period of

_____ to reach the required standard for entry to

the course. (know, revise)

Plastic surgery is expensive and might not bring about the

_____ you are hoping for. (transform)

(perspiration; confirmation; edition; reservation; length;
width; real; information; knowledge; revision; transformation)

Looking at the endings of words for meaning

We've looked at how words which are related may have a similar
spelling pattern. Looking at the endings of words may also tell us
something about their meaning and their spelling.

1 An ending which shows that a word is a verb

looked   whipped   kissed
commanded   landed   asked

These are verbs. They are 'doing' words. They tell you about an
action. These particular verbs all have –ed endings. They do not
share the same meaning but they have something very important in
common. They are all *past tense verbs*. They all mean an action
which happened in the past.
The –**ed** ending gives the meaning of *past*.

Example
Today I am going to plan my holiday. (Now, in the present)
Yesterday I plan**ned** my holiday. (Yesterday, in the past)
Last week I ask**ed** for a rise, but instead I was sack**ed**. (Last week,
in the past)

Spelling mistakes often occur in words which have –**ed** endings because of the sound the ending makes.

kicked		_kicked_
kissed	} –ed sounds like 't'	_____
walked		_____
jumped		_____

landed		_____
planted	} –ed sounds like 'id'	_____
acted		_____
committed		_____

robbed		_____
planned	} –ed sounds like 'd'	_____
killed		_____
shared		_____

When you are spelling these words
● don't think about the sound of their ending;
● think about their meaning – they tell you that something happened in the past.

Use the past tense of the verb in brackets to fill the gap in the line. The ending will always be –ed. If the word in brackets has to change before adding –ed, this is shown.

Until Dr Johnson _published_ his   (publish)

dictionary in 1755, most people _____   (spell)

as they spoke. If they _____ to   (want)

spell a word several different ways in the

same letter, no one who _____ (receive – drop 'e')

the letter really _____   (mind)

B

But Dr Johnson _____ all that. His   (spoil)

dictionary and those which _____ have   (follow)

_____ us into self-conscious perfectionists,   (turn)

_____ about our mistakes.   (worry – 'y' to 'i')

If the good doctor could have _____ (imagine – drop 'e')

the consequences of his having _____   (fix)

the spelling at that stage, he might

have _____ more people, and   (consult)

_____ a system of spelling which   (design)

was logical and simple.

What an opportunity _____ !   (waste – drop 'e')

Instead he _____ together all   (collect)

the spellings which were in use at that time,

and _____ them for posterity.   (record)

2 An ending which shows that a word is an adjective

Look at the words in italics. They are adjectives. They are used to describe things.

A *musical* instrument

A *medical* dictionary

A *critical* operation

Words which end in –cal are often confused with words ending in –cle (uncle; bicycle; particle) because they sound similar.

Rule When you hear the 'kl' sound at the end of a word, if the word is an adjective the ending is –cal.

Put the –cal adjectives below in an appropriate space.

focal; theatrical; logical; technical; vocal; optical; tropical; classical; alphabetical; identical; physical; political; practical; local; clinical; mechanical; vertical; topical

the _focal_ point

the _____ hospital

a _____ performance

a _____ solution

a _____ line

your _____ cords

a _____ college

a _____ examination

a _____ news item

a _____ argument

an _____ illusion

a _____ breakdown

_____ twins

_____ music

_____ order

_____ fitness

a _____ island

a _____ party

3 Some verb and noun endings

Nouns	*Verbs*
advice	advise
practice	practise
licence	license
device	devise
prophecy	prophesy

These pairs of words sound almost the same and have very similar meanings but they end with 'c' or 's' depending on whether they are nouns or verbs.

To decide whether to use 'c' or 's' you have to know exactly what you want the word to mean.

If you want to *name* something use a *noun* with 'c'.

If you want to explain what's happening, use a *doing word*, a *verb* with 's'.

Example advice – advise

These are the easiest to explain because they sound different

advice – noun

A consultant will give you advice

(advice is the *name* of what the consultant gives you)

advise – verb

A solicitor will advise you to sue

(advise is the word which tells you what the solicitor will *do*)

For nouns use 'c'

A consultant gives you advice.

A marriage guidance counsellor gives you _____

A doctor has his practice.

A clarinettist does his _____

You need a licence to drive a car.

To sell cigarettes and cigars you need a _____

For verbs use 's'

A solicitor will advise you to sue.

A specialist will _____ you to give up smoking.

A student must practise his spelling.
A singer must _____ her scales.

A magistrate will license you to sell alcohol.
James Bond 007 is _____ to carry a gun.

Note: If the word ends in **-ed** or **-ing** it must be a verb
  a practi**sed** liar, our licen**sing** laws.

Think about this

**Some people find this helpful. When you *s*ing a *c*arol, the
verb has an 's' and the noun has a 'c'. At *c*hoir practi*c*e you
practi*s*e *s*inging.**

Note
Practice and practise are used frequently throughout this book.
When practice is used it is the *name of the activity* (noun). When
practise is used it is describing what you have to do (verb).

USING THE MEANINGS OF WORDS

SOME OTHER USEFUL SKILLS

Good spellers are not always consciously thinking about rules, syllables, suffixes, etc. They have reached a stage where most of their spelling is automatic. Only when they're stuck do they stop and work out how a word is likely to behave. We reach this automatic stage with every skill we learn – if we get enough practice.

A learner driver thinks he'll never be able to co-ordinate all the hand, eye and foot movements involved in changing gear. The experienced driver has practised these separate operations until they happen as a smooth, co-ordinated movement which produces the right result.

Spelling is the same. A lot of knowledge and many skills have to be co-ordinated to produce the right word. In Parts A and B we dealt with the basic knowledge you need to improve your spelling. In Part C we shall learn the other skills good spellers use when they are operating at the 'automatic' level. These are the skills involved in 'just knowing when it's right':

C1   Knowing when a word looks right

C2   Knowing when a word feels right

We'll also look at what every writer does when all else fails:
C3   Using a dictionary.

KNOWING WHEN A WORD LOOKS RIGHT

Being able to tell when a word looks right or wrong is very important. You're half-way towards improving your spelling when you can spot your mistakes.

Even good spellers may have to write a word and look at it before they know if it's correct. Tests have shown that good spellers are skilled at remembering the visual appearance of words and the order in which letters occur. This is the skill you have to develop if your spelling is to improve. It involves three things:

● Learning to recognize the combination of letters which are likely to occur in English words.

● Training yourself to remember the look of whole words or chunks of words.

● Training yourself in the habit of looking at your writing for errors – proof-reading.

Learning which combinations of letters are likely to occur

Here's an experiment. Try it on your family and friends.

Sort these words into French, Russian and German.

spreintzel	essoiement	fillère
toskarovitch	Zeubermann	molenchev
tzarpov	föln	flugelhofen
étiolergé	niscoff	brôtissage

Did other people make the same decisions as you? What made you decide the way you did?

All these words were made up. They are not 'real' Russian, German or French words. They just look like those languages because they contain combinations of letters which are likely to occur in those languages. Every language has its own letter patterns which give that language its distinctive 'look' – strings of letters which make a language look familiar or foreign.

English is the same. There are strings of letters which give English its characteristic appearance. Good spellers have an eye for this. They might not know it consciously, but subconsciously when they work out a spelling they choose combinations of letters which are likely to occur in English. They know what English ought to look like. This means their spelling is more likely to be correct.

To be a good speller you have to be able to recognize when words look right or look wrong. To develop this skill you should pay close attention to the visual structure of words when you are learning them and you must use them in writing.

How can you learn to recognize letter patterns?

Collect together words which contain the same letter patterns so that you have lots of examples to study. In that way your eye will become 'tuned in' to the pattern. If you are to learn the word HEIGHT, make yourself aware of the –eigh– pattern by listing other words which contain that string of letters.

height _height_		sleigh	
eight		neighbour	
sleight		Leigh on Sea	
freight		weigh	

These words share the same *visual pattern* – they look the same. They don't all sound the same. When making a group of words do it by looking at the letters, not by listening to the sound they make.

Here are two more letter patterns:

chatter	*chatter*	act	*act*
pattern	_____	practice	_____
scattered	_____	actor	_____
batter	_____	react	_____
battery	_____	action	_____
matters	_____	practical	_____
flattery	_____	factual	_____
splatter	_____	attractive	_____

In virtually every word in English there is a letter pattern which could also be found in other words. Look out for these patterns and you will be training your 'spelling eye'. On the following pages are puzzles to help you to focus on the letter patterns in some words which cause problems for writers.

Did you know?

English is the first language of 350 million people in the world; people of many nationalities and with widely different accents. Three-quarters of the world's mail, telex and cables is written in English.

WORDSEARCH

Can you find fifteen words with the -sci- letter string? All the words at the bottom of the page are in each wordsearch puzzle. Write over the words as you find them. We have highlighted two for you.

```
W S C I E N T I S T O V H S
U Y S C I M I T A R M F X C
N S C I N T I L L A T E P I
C O S C I E N T I F I C S E
O G S M S C I S S O R S I N
N G G F T V C E K O E T Z C
S U T I Q O S C I L L A T E
C O N S C I E N T I O U S R
I Q B O V K C A J G I O H L
O C O N S C I E N C E O Y O
U S U N C O N S C I O U S W
S P S D I S C I P L I N E B
S C I O N S C I A T I C A O
J D I S C I P L E V O Z C E
```

```
Q Y G W U O C J S C I O N N
J Z S C N B O D Y C Q G R Z
S F C O C S N E T A I L V S
C S I N O D S Y D N U O C C
I C E S N I C J I M N S N I
M I N C S S I S S R C C O E
I N T I C C E C C S O I S N
T T I E I I N I I C N S C T
A I F N O P T E P I S S I I
R L I C U L I N L A C O L S
W L C E S I O C E T I R L T
G A J Y O N U E Q I O S A N
U T N E P E S S V C U J T A
D I S C I P L E M A S E E G
```

conscience (as in guilty conscience)   disciple   scintillate (to sparkle or twinkle)   science   discipline   scissors   scientist conscious (awake with all your senses working)   scion (a piece cut off a plant for grafting)   scientific   unconscious   oscillate (to swing from side to side)   conscientious (serious about your work) sciatica (rheumatism of the hip)   scimitar (a curved sword)

WORDTOWER

All the words below contain the –wor– letter pattern

It's built up of letters

A legless slimy creature

Effort

To take the oath; to be . . . . . in

Past tense of swear

A long, sharp weapon

If you're not better, you're . . . . .

The most bad

Value

Anxiety

To adore

The Earth

With all my . . . . goods
I thee endow

Honest and reliable

Sauce named after a town
in the West Midlands

C

worry; trustworthy; work; worm; worse; word; sword; worldly;
swore; worship; worth; worst; world; sworn; Worcester

CROSSWORD

Every answer is a word which contains the –ough– letter string.

Across

3 The past tense of 'fight'
5 Town with a municipal corporation
6 The past tense of 'buy'
8 Attentive to detail
9 A sugary bun with a hole in it
13 The opposite of smooth
14 A town in Essex
16 A piece of farm machinery
17 0, the number
18 The past tense of 'seek'
19 The past tense of 'bring'
20 The past tense of 'think'

Down

1 Caused by a tickle in the throat
2 There's plenty of this in a high-fibre diet
4 Opposite of 'tender'
6 Branch of a tree
7 Manager of Nottingham Forest Football Club
9 Unbaked bread
10 Pigs eat out of this
11 A very dry spell with no rain
12 Sufficient
15 A town in Bucks

Answers
1 cough   **2** roughage   **3** fought   **4** tough   **5** borough
6 (*across*) bought   **6** (*down*) bough   **7** Brian Clough
8 thorough   **9** (*across*) doughnut   **9** (*down*) dough
10 trough   **11** drought   **12** enough   **13** rough
14 Loughton   **15** Slough   **16** plough   **17** nought
18 sought   **19** brought   **20** thought

Training yourself to remember whole words
Research into spelling has shown that the people who are good
spellers are usually those with good visual memory. They can easily
recall what words look like and can remember the order in which
the letters come. They can tell at a glance whether words look right
or wrong.

Fortunately this is a skill which can be developed – if you are
determined.

What do you do?
If you want to remember whole words you have to study whole
words.
● Pick a word you can see now, on this page, or in a newspaper,
or on the coffee jar, anywhere within view.
● Look at it closely for a few seconds and try to build up a mental
picture of the whole word.
● Say it to yourself as you study it.
● Now, *without looking back at the word*, write it in this box.

(It's important that you don't look back until you've finished,
because this will interfere with your picture of the *whole* word.)
● If you get stuck, cross it out.
● Look back at the original, but this time concentrate on the part
you got wrong. Back up your visual memory by talking to yourself
about the part of the word you have to remember.
● Try it again.

C

● Do this until you can visualize the whole word and reproduce it correctly in writing.

Try it with the adverts on television.

Advertisers helpfully flash up clearly printed, colourful words onto the screen and leave them there a few seconds for you to study – they *want* you to learn the words.

Look closely at the word while it's on the screen and say it to yourself.

When the word disappears test yourself to see how much you can remember.

Check your result when the word reappears as it inevitably does – advertisers know that repetition is essential if you want a viewer to remember the brand names.

The words around us in shops, on signs, on posters, are ideal for training the visual memory. They have been designed by people who want to capture our attention by visual means, people who are specialists in presenting information in a way which catches the eye and fixes a picture on the brain.

Use their skills to train your skills.

Training yourself to proof-read
This is the final 'Does it look right?' check of your written work.

When you have finished a piece of writing you need to stand back from it for a moment and then look at it with a fresh eye. Many mistakes are made when getting ideas onto paper because you're concentrating on what you want to say. This is as it should be. You don't want to be held up checking the details of spelling when you're writing out first rough drafts – that would slow you down and spoil the flow. Therefore it's very important that you look closely at the work before it leaves you and goes to some other reader.

It is easier to spot mistakes if you read your work aloud. This will slow you down and make you listen to what you've written. It will also force you to look more closely at individual words.

Look for the following things
● First, and most important, check that the writing makes sense and says what you want it to say.
● Check the punctuation. At least make sure the full stops are in the right places.
● Check for missing words. When you're writing quickly to get your ideas down on paper, your mind is ahead of your hand and words may get left out.
● Check the endings of words – 's' and 'ed' are often left off. It's as if the hand is satisfied with the base word without its ending and the mind and eye have already moved on to the next word without checking.
● Look for words you know you may get wrong, like homophones – check that you've used 'their' or 'there' correctly.
● If a word looks doubtful, check it with a dictionary. Check for specific problem areas like double letters or 'ei'/'ie' words.

Final point about proof-reading
Don't proof-read for everything at the same time. Select one item for checking and read through, searching specifically for that. For example, read through looking for missing endings, then read again for words where double letters might be a problem.

Think about this

You might not be able to correct all your mistakes but, if you don't proof-read your work, someone else may spot the mistakes you could have dealt with.

KNOWING WHEN A WORD FEELS RIGHT

It may sound ridiculous to say that good spellers know when a spelling feels right. You can test it by quickly writing a word you know you always spell correctly. Try writing your name in your usual handwriting.

_____

Easy wasn't it? Now write it again, at the same speed but try spelling it wrongly – leave out some letters, or put them in the wrong order.

_____

Doesn't it *feel* wrong? It takes effort and concentration to *stop* your hand producing the correct movements it has learned to make automatically.

When you write familiar spellings your hand seems to remember the movement it has to make in order to produce the right letters in the right order. You have the right spelling at your finger tips. It's the same sort of memory that's used when knitting or playing the piano. The person who is skilled at these things has learned a series of well co-ordinated physical movements which they use fast and fluently, one movement leading to the next, producing a sequence of movements which gives the correct result.

Typists can do it too. Through practice they learn a set of finger movements which produce a particular spelling. People who do a lot of typing may tell you they can spell better on a typewriter than with a pen. This is because they have had more practice in the movements which produce correct spelling on a typewriter.

```
I can spell on a manual typewriter


I can spell on an electric typewriter


I can spell on a word processor
```

Type to spell
If you do most of your writing on a typewriter, you should practise
your spellings on a keyboard using the fingering you have learned
in your typing lessons. If you have your own method of fingering,
which you always use, stick to that.

Write to spell
If you will be writing by hand as most of us do, then practise your
spellings in your own fluent, joined-up handwriting. Practise over
and over again until the letters run from your fingers, through the
pen and onto the paper. Practise each word until you can do it with
your eyes closed. But first make sure your handwriting is efficient
enough to let your hand learn the easy, fluent hand movements
which are important if you are to improve your spelling.

What is efficient handwriting?

As far as this book is concerned, a handwriting style is efficient if it
is helpful to you in learning to spell. This means that
● the letters will slope more or less in the same direction so that
you can build up speed and fluency;
● it won't have capital letters in the middle of words because, in
addition to being wrong, this interrupts the flowing movement
when you write (there are hardly any exceptions to this; the best
known ones are Scottish surnames such as McDonald);
● in each word the letters will be evenly sized and spaced and in
many cases they will be joined up so that you can glide easily from
one letter to the next;

- it will be clear enough to give a good visual picture of the words you are trying to remember;

b d f h k l t will be taller than a c e m w

f g j p q will have tails which go below the line of writing;

t s will be crossed and i s will be dotted;

- it will be legible to other people if and when you want them to read it!

Efficient handwriting need not be beautiful, or even neat. It should be relaxed and easy to produce without your hand becoming tired or cramped. It should also be fairly fast so that you can build up smooth continuous patterns. Some examples are shown below.

Spelling it out   Spelling it out

Spelling it out   Spelling it out

If you don't have fast efficient handwriting you can improve it by
- noticing what's wrong with your present style;
- deciding which aspects you want to improve;
- practising writing.

Practise your handwriting on *correct* spellings. Never, never practise writing a word which is wrongly spelled. If you do, your hand and eye will learn and remember the wrong pattern.

When you are learning a word, always check back to the original correct spelling before you test yourself. This is not cheating. It's the best way to learn. You are reinforcing your mental picture of the correct spelling. Your hand will be more likely to produce the letters in the right order and you will have learned the word more effectively.

Think about this

You've probably been practising wrong spellings for years. No wonder it's so difficult to 'unlearn' them!

C3

USING A DICTIONARY

A dictionary is the most useful book a learner speller can possess. Not only does it give the spelling but some will tell you everything you need to know about a word; how to pronounce it; its various meanings; how to break it into syllables; the words which can be built up from it; which language the word came from.

Unfortunately, when all this information is included, it makes the dictionary difficult to use. You often have to decipher all the abbreviations. There's some help with this on the next page.

But first you have to find your word. The one thing all dictionaries have in common is that the words are arranged in alphabetical order. There is a section for each letter from A to Z. Within each section the words are arranged alphabetically. **Fable** comes before **face** because 'b' comes before 'c' in the alphabet.

At the top of each page there are usually two guide words:

beetle	61	behind

beetle³ /'biːt(ə)l/ **1** *a.* projecting, shaggy, scowling (*beetle brows*). **2** *v.i.* project, overhang (*beetling cliff*). [orig. unkn.]

beetroot *n.* red root of garden beet, used as vegetable. [BEET]

befall /bɪ'fɔːl/ *v.* (*past* **befell**; *p.p.* **befallen**) happen (to). [OE (BE-)]

befit /bɪ'fɪt/ *v.t.* (-tt-) be suited to, be proper for. [BE-]

nearest boundary *at* (*Asia begins at the Bosphorus*). [OE]

beginner *n.* one who is just beginning, esp. to learn a skill; **beginner's luck** good luck supposed to attend a beginner.

beginning *n.* first part of thing; time or place at which thing begins; source, origin; **beginning of the end** first clear sign of (esp. unfavourable) outcome.

The word on the left is the first word on the page. The word on the right is the last word. When you're flicking through the pages looking for a word you'll be able to tell if it comes between the two guide words. You can then scan down the columns of words until you spot what you're looking for.

If you can't find your word it might be that you're looking for the wrong first letter. On pages 38–40 is a list of alternative ways of making initial sounds. This may help you.

The italic letter after the word shows which part of speech the word is. **spell**[1] *n.* is a noun, **spell**[2] *v.* is a verb, **spell**[3] *n.* is a noun.

The word **spell** appears three times with a number next to each word. This is because the three words all have different origins although they are now all spelled the same.

The letters in square brackets at the end of the entry show which language the word comes from. **spell**[1] [OE] comes from Old English. **spell**[2] [F f. Gmc, rel. to prec.] means we get this word from French (F) which took it from (f) a Germanic (Gmc) language. It is related (rel) to the preceding (prec) entry. The preceding entry is **spell**[1]. This means that the origin of **spell**[2] is linked to the origin of **spell**[1].

If a word can be used as more than one part of speech this is shown with a bold number. **spell**[3] **1** *n.* can be used, firstly, as a noun (a period of time) and, secondly, **2** *v.t.*, as a verb (to take turns).

This information in brackets tells you that that past tense of this word can be either **spelt** or **spelled** (His name was spelt (or spelled) wrongly on the form).

The rest of the information is the definition or word meaning. Sometimes several, slightly different meanings are given.

For extra clarity the word is sometimes used in a phrase or sentence.

spell¹ *n.* words used as charm or incantation etc.; effect of these; fascination exercised by person or activity. [OE]

spell² *v.* (*past* & *p.p.* **spelt** or **spelled**) write or name correctly the letters of (word); (of letters) make up (word); (of circumstances etc.) have as consequence, involve (*floods spell ruin to the farmer*); **spell out** make out (words etc.) laboriously or slowly, spell aloud, explain in detail. [F f. Gmc. rel. to prec.]

spell³ 1 *n.* period of time or work; period of some activity (*a spell of resting*); period of certain type of weather (*cold spell*). 2 *v.t.* relieve or take turns with (person etc.). [OE, = substitute]

spellbound *a.* held as if by a spell, fascinated. [SPELL¹]

spelling *n.* way word is spelt, esp. correctly; person's ability to spell correctly. [SPELL²]

spelt¹ *n.* a kind of wheat giving very fine flour. [OE]

spelt² see SPELL².

This shows that the words **spelling** and **spelt** are related to the second word **spell**.

C

Not all dictionaries are the same. Some are more complex than the one we've shown, others are much simpler, and others use the same conventions (of numbering etc.) but in different ways. The simplest of all are alphabetic word lists with no meanings.

length	how long something is from one end to the other	
lengthen	to make longer	**lengthened** **lengthening**
lens	a circular piece of glass for bending light	**lenses**

BENTWOOD CHAIR

bentwood (bent′wood′) *adj.* designating furniture made of wood permanently bent into various forms by heat, moisture, and pressure

beriberi (ber′ē ber′ē) *n.* [Singh. *beri*, weakness] a deficiency disease caused by lack of thiamine (vitamin B₁) in the diet
berk (burk) *n.* [< *Berkshire Hunt*] [Slang] a stupid person; fool
berkelium (bur′klē əm) *n.* [< University of California at *Berkeley*] a radioactive chemical element: symbol, Bk
Berks. Berkshire
Bermuda shorts (bər myōō′ də) [< island in W Atlantic] short trousers extending to just above the knee
berry (ber′ē) *n., pl.* ber′ries [OE. *berie*] 1. any small, juicy, fleshy fruit, as a raspberry, etc. 2. the dry seed of various plants, as a coffee bean 3. *Bot.* a fleshy fruit with a soft wall and thin skin, as the tomato, etc. —ber′rylike′ *adj.*

armada [ɑːˈmɑːdə] *n.* fleet of warships.
armadillo [ɑːməˈdɪləʊ] *n.* small South American animal covered with a flexible shell.
armageddon [ɑːməˈgedən] *n.* great final battle.
armature [ˈɑːmətjə] *n.* moving part of an electric motor; coil in a dynamo.

arsenal [ˈɑːsənl] *n.* store of weapons.
arsenic [ˈɑːsnɪk] *n.* (*element:* As) powerful poison.
arson [ˈɑːsn] *n.* criminal act of setting fire to a property. **arsonist,** *n.* person who sets fire to property.
art [ɑːt] *n.* painting, drawing, sculpture and music; **a. gallery** = museum of paintings, sculptures, etc.; **arts subjects** = subjects (such as

Before buying a dictionary you should try out a few and decide which you find easiest to work with. You might need more than one!

If you can't find the word you're looking for or you're not sure what an abbreviation means, it's a good idea to look at the dictionary's introduction. These introductions used to be highly academic and technical, but in new editions of dictionaries great efforts have been made to make them more readable.

TWENTY TIPS FOR ANXIOUS SPELLERS

Ten tips for getting by

1   Don't fight the system. Stop trying to sound out words which can't be sounded out. Use sounds as *part* of the clue, then look for other evidence.

2   Use a dictionary. Shop around for one you like the layout of and which gives you the amount of information you need.

3   Use the words around you. If you don't have a dictionary to hand there are plenty of other places to look for help. Telephone directories will give you the correct spellings of personal names; that's more than a dictionary would do. Street names and place names are listed alphabetically in Thomson's Local Directory.

   Yellow Pages are a great source of words. Look under 'Plumbers', for example, and in the ads you'll find words like installation, guaranteed, emergency, genuine, maintenance. Under 'Builders' you'll find extension, specification, submitted, contractor and even crazy. Or perhaps you have a mail order catalogue.

4   Letters which have been sent to you will give you 'faithfully' or 'sincerely'. And if they need a reply, they may contain some of the words you need to use. Bills will contain words like 'electricity', 'discount' – or 'overdue'!

   Words are everywhere: on the cornflakes packet, the jam jar, on the front of your T-shirt. They come through the letter-box in the form of unsolicited mail. Keep your eyes open; you'll find the word you're looking for somewhere.

5   Keep lists of personally important spellings in a diary or note-book and carry it with you.

D

6   For tight spots have a piece of paper and pen handy. Pass them to the other person and say 'Would you just jot that down for me, please?'

7   Have a set approach for dealing with forms. 'I'll take this with me and complete it when I've had time to read it thoroughly – unless *you'd* like to do it for me now?'

8   When you're writing anything keep a separate piece of paper at your side for trying out words until you find one which looks right. This will stop your work getting cluttered with crossings out.

9   If you're writing something important, do a rough draft first and work that over before doing a neat copy. Proof-read your final effort. Read it as if you were the person receiving it. Look out for missing letters and full stops, endings left off and words which look wrong. Check any doubtful words in a dictionary.

10 Ask someone for the spelling. You never know, you might get the right answer. And if you don't, you'll make a whole new set of friends with the same problems as you!

Ten tips for getting better

1 Make a list of some words you know you can't spell and find a way of learning each one. Either write the word repeatedly until the pattern is fixed in your hand and eye, or invent a memory link (mnemonic) for reminding you of the spelling.

2 Attack words with many weapons. Split them up. Look for prefixes and suffixes. Play about with words by adding on new beginnings and endings. Think of other words which are from the same root or base. Play *Scrabble*; play *Lexicon*.

3 Learn words in groups which have the same letter pattern so that your eye becomes accustomed to what looks right, and your hand learns the patterns which regularly crop up.

4 Learn words in groups which follow the same rule. Don't bother to learn the rule; practise the words. The rule will 'click' with you eventually.

5 Think about the words you are learning and others which are related to them. Use your dictionary as an encyclopedia; it will show you how families of words are built up.

6 Read newspapers, magazines, cereal packets – not to notice the spelling, you'll read too quickly for that. Read to increase your vocabulary, to build up your knowledge of language and to develop a feeling for words and what they look like.

7 Notice the words around you, in shops, on buses, in newspaper headlines. Notice how they are built up. Learn to recognize how parts of one word might look like parts of another.

8 Write. Write often. Write anything.

9 Practise your handwriting. You'll like the look of your work much more and you'll find it easier to learn the letter patterns.

10 Look at your own writing. Identify your mistakes. Decide what you're doing wrong. Decide what you're going to do about it.

If you feel you can't do all these things on your own – join a class.

D

ENGLISH SPELLING PAST AND PRESENT

This section is for people who want to know more about the English language and how it has developed to give us the spellings we have today. There are also some thoughts on the pros and cons of changing the spelling system to make it easier.

How the system evolved

Spelling problems vary considerably from one language to another. Chinese, for example, does not use letters to represent individual sounds but uses characters to represent a complete word or section of a word. Spanish, like English, uses the Roman alphabet but is relatively easy to spell because each letter or group of letters always stands for the same sound. There are so few complications or exceptions that, generally, if you can say a word you can spell it. German and some other languages have problems with word-endings (or *inflections*) but they follow rules that can be learned.

English is exceptional, because particular letters or groups of letters can be pronounced in so many different ways and particular sounds can be written with so many different arrangements of letters. Letters and sounds just do not seem to correspond in a straightforward way. For instance, the same letter *s* is used to represent the final sound in *cats* and *dogs*. If you say the words out loud you will hear the sounds are different: in *dogs* it is much more like a *z*. The collection of letters *entrance* can stand for two entirely different and unrelated words: one (with emphasis on the *en-*) meaning 'a way in'; the other (with emphasis on *-trance* to rhyme with *dance*) meaning 'to bewitch'. The words *pierce* and *weird* have the same vowel sound, although the *i* and *e* are used in a different order; and the group of letters *ough* represents a wide variety of sounds in *bough, cough, enough, though, through,* and so on.

There are many more difficulties, inconsistencies and apparently pointless alternatives. Why *fitted* with double *t* but *benefited* with only one? Why *harass* with one *r* but *embarrass* with two? Why *questionnaire* with two *n*s but *millionaire* with only one? Why *proceeding* but *preceding*? Then there are all those confusing pairs of words that are spelt nearly the same way and yet have very different meanings, such as *there* (as in *over there*) and *their* (as in *lost their way*), or *stationary* (not moving) and *stationery* (paper and envelopes).

The mixed origins of English

Why then is our spelling so difficult? It is often thought that the number of words in the English language is a major reason, but this is not the real answer. Certainly, there are over half a million words in the *Oxford English Dictionary*, but only about 10 000 (less than two per cent) are in general everyday use. A much stronger reason is the rich variety of sources from which English comes, sources that are due to the different peoples who have conquered or settled in parts of the British Isles over the past 1500 years, and knowing more about the way English has evolved over this period makes its difficulties easier to understand.

What do we mean by an 'English' word? Many words are English in the sense that they can be traced back to the Anglo-Saxons – *Germanic* tribes which settled in England from around the fifth century AD. They gave us many common words like *book* and *house*, *cat* and *dog*. Earlier still were the Celtic peoples, whose speech survives in Scottish and Irish Gaelic, in Welsh, and in the local languages of two extremities of the British Isles, Manx (in the Isle of Man) and Cornish. There is practically no Celtic influence in English (except in names of places such as *Brecon, Inverness* and *London*, and in many river names, such as *Avon, Thames* and *Trent*). This is because the Celts were forced back into the fringes of the British Isles by the Anglo-Saxon invaders, and there was little cultural interaction.

The next important influence on the main vocabulary of English came in the ninth and tenth centuries when much of the east side of England was in the hands of Danish invaders (Vikings), and England as a whole had a Danish king Cnut (Canute) for a time. The Danes had much more contact with the Anglo-Saxons than did the Celts, and their short period of occupation has left its mark in the number of Scandinavian (Old Norse) words taken into our

E

language. Many of these are still in use, such as *take* and *law*, names of parts of the body such as *leg* and *skull*, and other basic words such as *egg* and *window*. Many more Scandinavian words are preserved in some dialects of the east side of England, in place-names such as those ending in *-thwaite* and *-thorpe* (both meaning 'settlement') and in street-names ending in *-gate* (from the Old Norse *gata* meaning 'street') such as *Coppergate* in York.

The last time that England was successfully invaded was in 1066 when William of Normandy defeated the English king Harold at the Battle of Hastings. The arrival of the Normans brought a further decisive influence on the language – French. French, together with Italian, Spanish, Portuguese and Romanian, is known as a Romance language, and has its roots in Latin, especially in the spoken or 'vulgar' Latin that survived until about AD 600. For several centuries, French (in its regional Norman form) was the language of the aristocracy in England and a large number of French words came into the language. Many of these words are to do with government, like *justice, council* and *tax*, and many are abstract terms like *liberty, charity* and *conflict*.

The Normans also had an important effect on the spelling of English words. The combination of letters *cw-*, for example, was standardized in the Norman manner to *qu-*, so that *cwēn* became *queen* and *cwic* became *quik* (later *quick*). In this way the Englishness of many words was effectively 'disguised'. This process of altering new words to look or sound more like words already in use is a feature of English throughout its history.

This mixture of conquering peoples and their languages – Germanic, Scandinavian and Romance – has had a decisive effect on the way we write English today. The three elements make up the basic stock of English vocabulary, and each has kept many of its own practices of putting sounds into writing. The different grammatical complications of each element can be seen in the structure and endings of many words. Many of the ˍriable endings such as *-ant* and *-ent*, *-er* and *-or*, *-able* and *-ible*, that are so easy to confuse, exist because the Latin words on which they are based belonged to different types or *classes* of verbs and nouns, each of which had a different ending. For example, *important* comes from the Latin verb *portare* meaning 'to carry' (which belongs to one class) while *repellent* comes from the Latin verb *pellere* meaning 'to drive' (which comes from another class). *Capable* comes from a Latin word ending in *-abilis* while *sensible* comes from one ending in -*ibilis*, and so on. This causes particular difficulty in English because Latin grammar is not our grammar. It is not something we carry in our heads – unless we happen to have been taught (and can remember!) Latin for its own sake.

Most of the words taken into the language over the years were adopted either because there was a basic need for them and they were useful (as, for example, with the many legal and formal words used by the Norman administrators) or because they were preferable in some way to the words already in use. Often the old word disappeared altogether, like the Old English *niman* which was replaced by the Old Norse (Scandinavian) *taka* (meaning *take*), and the Old English *sige* which was replaced by a word derived from Old French, *victory*. In many cases, however, the new word and the old continued in use side by side on a roughly equal footing. This has produced pairs of words which are both in use today, like *shut* and *close* or *buy* and *purchase*, in which the second word of each pair is French in origin. Sometimes we have an even larger overlap, as with *commence* (from French), and *begin* and *start* (from Old English).

In the first years after the Norman Conquest many of the new words were used only by the ruling class and professionals associated with them, such as scribes and clerks. The language of the common people remained largely unaffected. It was the spread of literacy and the development of printing (about which I shall say more later) that brought the French words into more general use. Often these were technical words, or words with an 'official' ring, such as *commence* and *purchase*. The result was a mixture of *types* of words – a feature of Middle English (as English from the Norman conquest to about 1500 is called) and of modern English. For many meanings we now have a choice of 'formal' and 'informal' words, the formal ones often being used only in very specific situations. For example, the word *vendor* is used instead of *seller* only in the context of buying or selling houses (and then only because estate agents and solicitors use it). Many technical words from Latin, such as *appurtenance*, survive only in legal documents, to the great confusion of the layman.

Cultural influences
There are several other historical developments which have affected the growth of English, and several of these resulted in Latin and Greek having a further influence on the language.

E

The first of these was Christianity, which originated in and spread through the Roman Empire. Latin was the official language throughout the Empire which stretched from Syria in the east to Spain, England and Wales in the west, and it survived as a language of ritual (and for a time also of communication) in the western Christian Church. During the Middle Ages (c. AD1100–1500), education was largely in the hands of the Church, and boys were taught Latin partly so that they could chant and sing in religious rituals. This led to the survival of Latin long after it ceased to be an ordinary living language, and added to its influence on English.

The second development was the rediscovery in Europe of the culture and history of the Ancient Greek and Roman worlds. This began at the end of the Middle Ages and blossomed in the fifteenth to seventeenth centuries – the time referred to as the European *Renaissance*. Scholarship flourished and the language used by scholars and writers in all countries was Latin. It was during the Renaissance that words such as *genius, arena, specimen* and *stimulus* appeared in English. They are familiar and useful words but their Latin origins sometimes make them awkward to handle, as, for example, when we use them in the plural. There was also a tendency in the Renaissance to try to emphasize the Greek or Latin origins of words when writing them. This accounts for the *b* in *debt* (the earlier English word was *det*; in Latin it is *debitum*), the *s* in *isle* (earlier *ile*; *insula* in Latin), and the *p* in *receipt* (earlier *receit*; *recepta* in Latin).

The development of machines and technology in Britain from the eighteenth century onwards, followed by the electronic revolution of our own times, has also played a part in continuing the influence of Latin. It has been necessary to devise a stock of technical terms and Latin or Greek words have often been used as their base because they can convey precise ideas in easily combinable forms, as in *heli/copter, micro/scope* and *semi/circle*, while sounding sufficiently contrived and 'classical' to give the terms a special status or 'ring'. This has sometimes produced odd mixtures, like *television*, which is half Greek and half Latin, and *microchip*, which is half Greek and half Old English!

In recent times English speakers have come into contact with people from other parts of the world, through trade, the growth of the British Empire and improved communications generally. This contact has produced a rich supply of new words that are often strange in form. India, where the British first made their presence felt in the seventeenth century, has given us words like *bungalow, jodhpurs* and *khaki*. Usually these words have been altered to make them look more natural to English eyes (*bungalow*, for example, is spelt *bangalo* in its original Gujarati form). Even so, such words often still have very 'unEnglish' spellings. Examples from other parts of the world are *harem* and *mufti* (from Arabic), *bazaar* (from Persian), *kiosk* (from Turkish) and *anorak* (from Eskimo). From European countries we have acquired *balcony* (from Italian), *envelope* (from French), and *yacht* (from Dutch).

This process of adapting foreign words into the English language has always been highly unpredictable, and so the spelling is difficult and unpredictable too. Usage often recognizes this by turning (or *assimilating*) new words into forms that are already familiar. The word *picturesque*, which came into use in the eighteenth century, is a compromise between its French source *pittoresque* and the existing Middle English word *picture*, to which it is obviously related. Our word *cockroach* is a conversion of its Spanish source-word *cucaracha* into a pair of familiar words *cock* (a bird) and *roach* (a fish). It is simply a matter of convenience; cockroaches, of course, have nothing to do with cocks or roaches, but the association makes the word easier to remember and use.

There is often a further difficulty when we have to alter the endings of 'foreign' words, for example when we want to use them in the plural. The ending *-i* in particular is very unnatural in English. Should the plural be *-is* or *-ies*? There is also a large number of adopted nouns ending in *-o*, some of which come from the Italian (*solo*), some from Spanish (*armadillo*) and some from Latin (*hero*), and these also cause difficulties in the plural form. Verbs often need special treatment, as for example *bivouac* (from French, and before that probably from Swiss German) which needs a *k* in the past tense (*bivouacked*, not *bivouaced* which might be mispronounced), and *ski* (from Norwegian) where usage allows both *ski'd* and *skied* as past forms (though neither is satisfactory). All these examples illustrate how words adopted into English from differently constructed languages often simply do not fit, causing major problems of spelling.

The effect of printing on English spelling

From the fifteenth century, when the first printed books appeared, the written forms of English went through many changes. When the first printers – many of whom were foreign, especially Dutch –

E

started work producing books in English, they found many variations in spelling. The word *soldier*, for example, is first recorded in the forms *sauder* and *sawder* and went through various forms such as *soudior* and *sourdeour* before developing the more recognizable forms of *souldier* and *soldier*; the *Oxford English Dictionary* records over sixty forms divided into six groups! Even an apparently simple Old English word like *sell* ran into scores of variations in its different tenses. (For example, in the past tense we have *sealde, seelde, soulde*, etc., and eventually *sold*.)

These variations arose partly because consistency of spelling was not then regarded as important, and partly because – with the spread of literacy – more people were writing. This meant more of the *vernacular* or common language was being written, with individuals using their own systems of spelling – or no system at all. There was no attempt to standardize spelling throughout the country. As long as other people – for example, family, friends and local traders – could understand what you had written there was no reason to. It would have been impractical, however, for printers to allow themselves such freedom; in written material that had to reach a much wider audience a more consistent system had to be devised. So the variety of spellings was greatly reduced in the work printers produced, although it was not eliminated altogether. *Soldier*, for example, continued to show variations up to (and occasionally beyond) the seventeenth century.

In this way a good measure of uniformity was imposed on the spelling of words. This uniformity, however, was based as much on practical considerations of the printing process as on what seemed most 'correct' or suitable. It became common practice, for example, to add a final *e* to words to fill a line of print. Many early printers used rules from their own languages, especially Dutch and Flemish, when setting English into type. Caxton, the first English printer (1422–91), exercised an important influence and not always for the good. The unnecessary insertion of *h* in *ghost*, for example, is due to Caxton and the influence of Flemish printers (whose word was *gheest*), and the change had its effect on other words such as *ghastly*.

The early printers' arbitrary approach to spelling caused many problems that are still with us. Nevertheless, thanks to them the written form of English did begin to become less erratic. Meanwhile, the pronunciation of English was undergoing major changes of its own. The main change, which began in the fourteenth century during the lifetime of the poet Chaucer, was in the pronunciation of vowel sounds. It resulted in the reduction of the number of 'long' vowels (for example in *deed* as distinct from *dead*) from seven to the five which we know today (as you can hear in the words *bean, barn, born, boon* and *burn*). It also affected the pronunciation of other vowels: the word *life*, for example, was once pronounced as we now pronounce *leaf*, and *name* was pronounced as two syllables to rhyme with *farmer*. In many cases, as with *name*, the spelling did not change; this accounts for many of the 'silent' vowels at the ends of words today. The result of these developments was a growing difference between what was spoken and what was written.

The importance of dictionaries

One obvious effect of the development of printing was that it allowed the language to be recorded in dictionaries, and this might be expected to have had a considerable effect on the way words were used and spelt. However, listing words in alphabetical order with their spellings and meanings is a relatively recent idea. Shakespeare, for example, did not use a dictionary because there was none to use. In 1580, when Shakespeare was sixteen, a schoolteacher named William Bullokar did publish a manual for the 'ease, speed, and perfect reading and writing of English', and he also called for the writing of an English dictionary. But such a dictionary, the work of Robert Cawdrey (another schoolteacher), was not published until 1604. Like the dictionaries that then followed in quick succession, its purpose was described as being for the understanding of 'hard words'. It was not until the eighteenth century that dictionaries systematically listed all the words in general use at the time regardless of how 'easy' or 'hard' they were, and the most notable of these were compiled by Nathan Bailey (1721) and, especially, Samuel Johnson (1755). But even these dictionaries were full of inconsistencies, and some still did not even list the words in alphabetical order.

For all their faults, the new dictionaries played an important part in settling the spelling of words. Their influence, and again Johnson's in particular, is illustrated by the history of the word *dispatch*. Johnson inadvertently entered this in the form *despatch*, a spelling that he did not normally use and which was far less common. It has been so widely accepted in normal use since Johnson's time, however, that it is likely to survive and even to oust the 'correct' spelling.

E

The systematic investigation and recording of words in all their aspects is first and exclusively represented in the *Oxford English Dictionary*, begun by the Scottish schoolteacher James A. H. Murray in 1879. This describes the history, spelling and meaning of words, and includes quotes from printed literature and other sources as evidence from Old English to the present day. To keep up with changes and developments in the language a four-volume *Supplement* was added to the work from 1972 to 1986, and a new edition in which the two have been integrated into one is to be published shortly. Because of the depth of scholarship that went into this work, the *Oxford English Dictionary* forms a major basis of all English dictionaries produced since.

We should always remember, however, that dictionaries generally record the language as it is being used at the time, and with usage constantly changing the distinction between 'right' and 'wrong' is sometimes difficult to establish. Today's mistake can be tomorrow's alternative usage, as we saw with Johnson's *despatch*. In the meantime, editors of dictionaries have to identify what is 'wrong' on the basis of what seems to be harming the language and its usefulness. In the following list the first of each pair is the correct spelling and the second is a commonly found misspelling. The misspellings have arisen because the words sound like words with a different spelling.

attach	*attatch* (confused with *batch, dispatch*, etc.)
consensus	*concensus* (confused with *census*)
idiosyncrasy	*idiosyncracy* (confused with words like *democracy* etc.)
minuscule	*miniscule* (confused with *mini*)
mischievous	*mischievious* (confused with *devious*)
tranquillity	*tranquility* (confused with *agility, ability*, etc., where the root words *agile, able*, etc., do not already end in *l* – see page 69)

One can say then that these misspellings are 'wrong', but in other cases it is not so simple. The spelling of *on to* as a single word *onto* has long been deplored by purists but is now very common and seems quite acceptable. *Alright* for *all right* (similar to *altogether*) is also generally rejected but will undoubtedly be accepted eventually.

These remarks may not be very helpful if you are looking for hard and fast rules to help you master the spelling of English, but they are important if you want to get an idea of the way the language works and develops and to understand the part played by dictionaries. Unlike French, which is guided by the rulings of the *Académie Française*, there is no single authority in English to say whether a particular spelling is 'right' or 'wrong'; established usage is what matters. One result of this is that English tolerates many more alternative spellings than other languages. Dictionaries, therefore, sometimes differ in the spellings they adopt in individual cases: *enquire* is just as correct as *inquire*, *conjurer* as *conjuror*, *generalise* as *generalize*, and so on. The alternatives do not amount to a 'free for all' but are based on certain patterns of word formation and variation in the different languages through which they have passed before reaching ours.

Towards a more 'streamlined' English
Spelling depends on usage, and usage in modern times is greatly influenced by rapid worldwide communications, by newspapers and, in particular, by television and radio. Speakers of British English are brought into daily contact with alternative forms of the language, especially American English. American English often has more regular and sensible spellings, such as the substitution of *-er* for *-re* in words like *theatre*, the standardization of *-or* and *-our* to *-or* in words like *harbour*, and the use of *-se* in forms like *defense* and *license* where British English either has *-ce* only or both forms (for example, a *practice* but to *practise* – see page 82). This influence is often regarded as unsettling or harmful but there is no doubt that it will have some considerable effect on the spelling of British English, and is indeed already doing so.

There have been several attempts over the years to introduce spelling reforms to standardize written English and make it easier to learn. The most notable of these attempts was by George Bernard Shaw (1856-1950) who fought vigorously but unsuccessfully for the use of a new alphabet that could represent the sounds of English consistently. The proposed reforms, however, tend to produce as many complications as they remove. Shaw's alphabet, for example, requires over forty characters to stand for all the sounds involved. He left his fortune for the development of this and in 1962, twelve years after his death, his play *Androcles and the Lion* was published in the Shaw Alphabet. Here's an excerpt:

E

ANDROCLES [*whispering*] Did you see? A lion.
MEGAERA [*despairing*] The gods have sent him to
punish us because youre a Christian. Take me
away, Andy. Save me.

ᓴᑊᑐᖓᐦ [ᐱᔅᑐᕆᕆ] ᒧᒡ ᐃ Sᠲ? ᖪ ᖏᖂ.
ᓴᑐᖏᖓ [ᐱᔅᑐᕆᕆ] ᖫ ᑐᕆᕆ ᖕᖁᖓ Sᠲᕐ ᖟᕐ 1
]ᑌᖋᖤ 7S ᑌᒡᕆᖃ ᑭᐧᖏ ᖑ ᖏᕆᔅᑎᖏ. ᑎᕐᖚᖓ ᓭ
ᕐᐱᕐ, ᐧᖮᖐ. Sᕐᕐ ᓭ.

Others have proposed that 'superfluous' letters be removed, such as
the *e* in *blue* and the *b* in *bomb*. This sounds fine in principle but
other problems would remain (what about *tomb*, for example, which
has a different vowel sound?). What's more, such minor changes to
the language would undoubtedly meet fiercer public resistance than
did the recent conversion to metric weights and measures! The
spelling of English – with all its difficulties – is historically deeply
rooted in the language. It is therefore arguably an essential part of
it.

   These are some ways, then, in which the particular difficulties of
English spelling can be explained in terms of the history and
development of the language. Over the years words are battered
about as they pass from language to language and from one set of
users to another. The great strength of English, to my mind, is that
this process usually enriches and stimulates the language far more
than it threatens it or compromises it. Correct spelling means
respecting established usage far more than it means obeying fixed
and unchangeable rules, and that is a mark of a living and
flourishing language.

Should we change the system?

One of the arguments in favour of change is that spelling would be easier and more logical if every sound had its own letter and if every word could be spelled exactly as it sounds. This is true; it would make writing much easier. But it is not as simple as it seems.

● The same word doesn't always sound the same. Words will sound different when they are in different places in a sentence and when different stress is put upon them.
Say these sentences:
Have you had a rise? I have.
You should have had a rise.
When you speak these words naturally the word 'have' sounds different each time.
Would it really be sensible to spell these words differently when they sound different?

● What about words which change their sound when you add endings to them?
'Sign' becomes 'signal' with a 'g' sound when you add –al.
'Medic' becomes 'medicine' with an 's' sound when you add –ine.
Doesn't it make sense for these words to keep their basic spelling even when they change their sound? If they look the same, we can see they belong together and have a similar sort of meaning.

● What about the pronunciation used by people from different parts of the country? Will the sheep farmer from the Yorkshire Dales have to spell his 'grass' differently from the cricketer in Surrey, just because he says it differently?
We have many different accents in the British Isles but we can read each other's letters because we share the same spellings for words. If we all decided to spell words according to how we say them, there would be chaos. We would never be able to communicate in writing.
If the spelling system was changed so that it represented the way we speak, whose accent should it match, yours or mine? Mine of course!

● Finally, what about the hundreds of words in English which sound the same but look different?
bare bear;   meet meat;   see sea;   find fined

If we spelled words as they sound, all homophones would look the same. Think how confusing this would be to read. Try this:

a   eye grown two sea the wait eye mite have two bare.

Now try this:

b   I groan to see the weight I might have to bear.

The sentences sound the same because the main words are all homophones. But wasn't **a** more difficult to read than **b**?

In **a** the *appearance* of the words was giving a message that didn't make sense. You were picking up a confusing meaning through your eyes even before you heard the sound of the words. You have to slow down and turn the words into sound in order to try to make sense of the sentence. The only way to make sense of it is by ignoring what the words look like. In **b** the appearance of the words was giving a message which made sense. You didn't need to turn the words into sounds so the reading was quicker and easier.

It is helpful to the reader if the 'look' of a word gives clues about its meaning. It speeds up the reading if you can pick up the meaning at a glance, without having to hear the sound of the words. So, if we removed the visual clues by making all homophones look the same, reading would be more difficult. Perhaps spelling by sound is not as simple a solution as it first seems.

Last thoughts about the spelling system

The system we have is good for the reader, especially the fluent reader. The way words are spelled makes it easy to see the meanings quickly. It's not so good for a beginning reader who's trying to work out a lot of new words. It's particularly bad for spellers. But it's worst of all for spellers who try to work out spellings from the sounds of words only. That's not how the system is designed to work. It's not intended to show you what the language sounds like.

Our spelling system is designed for people who speak the language and who know about how words are linked together and built up. It shows you what words mean and where words come from. It will teach you about the English language – how words are related; which languages words come from. It will tell you something about our history – who conquered us, where we built an empire, where we traded, who came to settle in this country. If you want to be a good speller you have to take an interest in all this.

GLOSSARY OF TERMS

ADJECTIVE (page 80)
An adjective is a word which gives more information about a **noun**.

E.g. A *political* party (*political* is an adjective which describes the sort of party you have in mind); the *correct* spelling; *fluent* hand-writing; *careless* mistakes.

ALPHABETICAL ORDER (page 97)
When words are listed in alphabetical order they are arranged so that the first letters of the words are in the same order as the letters of the alphabet.

E.g. **apply   believe   catch   daughter   heavy   people**

If the first letters are the same, the words are put in order according to the second letter.

E.g. **settle   sincerely   strike   success   sweat   syllable**

If the second letters are the same, look at the third letter to decide the order, and so on.

APOSTROPHE (page 27)
An apostrophe is a mark (') used above a word to show that one or more letters have been left out.

E.g. *don't* – the apostrophe shows that the **o** of **not** has been left out when the words **do not** are run together.

they've – this is short for **they have**. The apostrophe shows that **ha** has been left out of **have**.

The apostrophe is also used to show ownership.

E.g. *Mary's briefcase* – the briefcase belongs to Mary so the apostrophe goes after Mary.

The ladies' cloakroom – the cloakroom belongs to the ladies, so the apostrophe goes after ladies.

The apostrophe is the most wrongly used punctuation mark. If you want to be sure of using it correctly get some help from a punctuation text book (see page 128).

CONSONANT (page 18)

All the letters of the alphabet are consonants *except* the 5 which are **vowels** 'a, e, i, o, u'. The letter 'y' can be a vowel or a consonant. At the beginning of words and syllables it is almost always a consonant – *yellow, yes, beyond.*

CONSONANT BLEND (page 40)

Where two or three consonants follow each other in a word they often slide or blend into one another so that it's difficult to say or hear them separately.

E.g. co**nn**ect, O**ct**ober; **scr**atch, de**scr**ibe; **tr**easure, re**tr**eat.

If you're having difficulty spelling a particular consonant blend, make a list of words which contain that blend and learn them together.

HOMOPHONES (page 23)

Homophones are words which sound the same but have different meanings.

E.g. sun – son; need – knead; plane – plain; night – knight; to – too – two; here – hear.

Don't learn them together – you'll confuse yourself even more.

MNEMONIC (page 13)

A mnemonic is a device to help your memory. It may be a rhyme to help you remember a spelling.

E.g. 'There's *end* on the end of fri*end*'.

Or it may simply be a knot in your handkerchief to remind you to do something.

NOUN (page 82)
A noun is a word which names an object, a place, a person or a feeling.

E.g. spanner; Southend; Peter; sadness.

PAST TENSE (page 78)
You use the past tense of a **verb** when you want to show that something has already happened.

E.g. She *had finished* her business so she *went* home early.

PLURAL (page 49)
This means more than one of anything.

E.g. Two *women* – *women* is the plural of *woman*.
Several *occasions* – *occasions* is the plural of *occasion*.

PREFIX (page 55)
A prefix is a **syllable** (or two syllables) added to the beginning of a word to change its meaning.

E.g. un (prefix)+necessary=unnecessary
anti (prefix)+freeze=antifreeze.

There is a list of prefixes on page 56.

PROOF-READING (page 92)
When something is being printed for publication the printer will first of all make one copy which he carefully checks for mistakes. This copy is called the *proof.*

The process of reading the proof to correct any errors before finally going to print, is called proof-reading. All writers need to proof-read their work before making it public.

PUNCTUATION (page 93)
Punctuation marks are used by writers to show a reader exactly how to interpret what's been written.

Full stops show where sentences end. *Commas* show how sentences are broken up into logical sections. *Quotation marks* show when someone is speaking. *Question marks* show the writer is making a query.

This book has not dealt with punctuation but if you want your writing to be read and understood by others, punctuation must be mastered. There are many useful and inexpensive punctuation books available (see page 128).

ROUGH DRAFT (page 92)
No one's writing is perfect at the first attempt. When you are concentrating on sorting out the best way to express your ideas, you are bound to make mistakes.

Rough draughts are the writer's early attempts at getting things right. They contain alterations, crossings-out, spelling and punctuation mistakes and they probably end up as crumpled bits of paper on the floor around you.

Rough draughts are private. No one needs to see them but the writer. However, they can be very useful in showing the type of mistakes you make and the sort of things you need to learn.

STRESS (page 66)
In this book we use the word 'stress' to mean the emphasis put on a certain part of a word when you say it.

E.g. **par**tly – stress is on 'par'
victim – stress is on 'vic'

sin**cere**ly – stress is on 'cere'
ad**vice** – stress is on 'vice'

SUFFIX (page 59)
A suffix is a syllable (or two syllables) added to the end of a word to change its meaning.

sincere+ly (suffix)=sincerely
beauty+ful (suffix)=beautiful

There is a list of suffixes on page 59.

SYLLABLE (page 17)
A syllable is the smallest part of a word which makes an individual sound when spoken aloud.

in=1 syllable
inside=2 syllables (in – side)
insider=3 syllables (in – side – er)

VERB (page 82)
A verb is a *doing* word. It tells you what's happening.

E.g. He *bathed* the baby and *put* her to bed.

Every sentence must have at least one verb.

E.g. It *rained.* I *go.*

VISUALIZE (page 92)
Visualizing means seeing a visual picture in your mind's eye. It's very important in spelling. You can train yourself to visualize by looking closely at words, or other objects, closing your eyes and picturing them in your mind.

VOWEL (page 18)
There are five vowels in the alphabet: a, e, i, o, u. All the other letters are **consonants**. y is a vowel when it does *not* begin a word or syllable: day; company; sympathy.

Every word has at least one vowel.
Act/**u**/**al**/ly, **each** syl/la/ble **has** at least **one** vow/el.

WORDLIST

accelerator
accent
accompaniment
ache
achieve
acid
acne
across
act
acted
action
actor
actual
address
admiration
admire
admitting
adorable
adoration
adore
adventurer
adventurous
advertize
advice
advise
all right
allies
allot
allotment
allotted
allotting
almost
alone
alphabetical

already
alright
also
alter
alteration
altering
although
altogether
always
annul
annulled
annulment
antecedent
antenatal
anteroom
anticlimax
antifreeze
anxiety
anxious
any
anywhere
apartment
apologize
appliance
application
applied
apply
applying
Arctic
argument
arithmetic
arrange
arrangement
arranger

asked
assign
assignation
Atlantic
atomic
attic
attractive
audible
audience
author
authority
autobiography
autograph
automatic
awful
badge
banjos
bare
barely
batter
battery
bear
beautiful
become
beggar
begged
begging
begin
beginner
beginning
believable
believe
benefited
between

bicycle
bigger
biggest
bomb
bombard
bombardier
borough
bough
bought
brief
brought
budget
budgeted
budgeting
buffaloes
burial
buried
burying
busier
busiest
business
busy
busying
buyer
calves
cameos
cancelled
capable
cared
careful
careless
cargoes
caring
carpenter

carriage	conference	deployed	eiderdown
carried	conferred	deployment	eight
carrying	conferring	designate	eighteen
catch	confirm	designed	eighty
ceiling	confirmation	designer	either
central	congratulations	despatch	electric
century	connect	detect	electrician
changeable	conscience	device	elves
chatter	conscientious	devise	embarrass
chemist	conscious	diarrhoea	employed
chief	conservative	dictionaries	employee
chiefs	consignment	dictionary	employer
chose	consulted	die	employment
Christmas	contain	diesel	emptied
cigarette	contract	digestive	empties
circle	contraction	disable	emptiness
city	contractor	disappear	empty
civil	convenience	disarmament	emptying
civility	conversation	disciple	emu
civilize	conveyance	discipline	encouraged
class	cottage	discomfort	encouragement
classic	cough	disease	encouraging
classical	courageous	disembark	endurance
clearly	critic	disgrace	enlarge
cliffs	critical	dishonest	enlarged
collar	criticize	dishonour	enlargement
collected	cry	dispatch	enlarger
college	cuckoos	display	enlarging
combination	cupful	disrupt	enough
combine	cyclone	dissatisfied	enrol
comic	cyst	dissent	enrolled
commanded	daily	disservice	enrolling
commit	damnation	dissolve	enrolment
commitment	dancing	div	ensign
committal	dawn	domestic	ensignia
committed	decay	dominoes	entrance
committee	deceit	donkeys	enviable
committing	deceive	doughnut	envied
companies	decide	drought	envious
conceited	decided	each	equal
concertos	declaration	echoes	equality
concrete	declare	edge	equalize
condemn	definite	edit	equalled
condemnation	delaying	edition	equip
confer	denial	editor	equipment

equipped	followed	gradual	hypocrite
equipping	forbid	gradually	ice
excellence	forbidden	grateful	identical
excellent	forbidding	gratefully	ignoble
exceptions	forceful	gratitude	illegal
exclude	foreign	grief	illegible
exit	foreigner	grievance	illegitimate
expel	forfeit	grieve	illogical
expensive	forget	halves	imagined
experience	forgetful	handful	imbalance
exploration	forgetting	handkerchiefs	imbibe
explore	forgive	happen	immature
export	forgiveness	happier	immediately
extended	forgotten	happiest	immigrant
eyeful	formal	happily	immobile
fact	formality	happiness	immoral
factories	formalize	harass	immovable
factual	forty	hateful	important
faithful	forward	have	impossible
faithfully	fought	hear	impress
fanciful	fourteen	heard	improper
fantastic	freight	hearing	improve
farmer	friend	hearsay	improved
fatless	frying	heavier	improvement
fatness	gaily	heaviest	inappropriate
fatter	garage	height	inaudible
February	garden	helpful	include
field	general	here	incompetent
fierce	generous	hereabouts	incorrect
final	gentleness	hereafter	indecent
finality	ghastly	hereby	indifferent
finalize	ghetto	herein	indigestible
finish	ghost	herewith	inexcusable
finite	ginger	heroes	infinite
fit	give	hoofs	inflamed
fitment	given	hooves	inflammable
fitted	giving	hoped	inflammation
fitter	gladden	hopeful	influence
fittest	gladness	hopeless	inform
fitting	glue	hoping	information
fixed	gnash	horrific	inhuman
flattery	gnome	houseful	inland
flyer	gorgeous	housing	inlay
flying	government	huge	inlet
focal	grade	hypocrisy	inmate

inmost	landed	managing	nervous
innocent	lazing	manful	niece
innumerable	lazy	manly	noisy
innumerate	leaves	manners	noticeable
inroad	legacy	mannish	noticed
inrush	legal	many	noticing
insignia	legality	market	nought
international	legalize	marketed	nowhere
interrogate	leisure	marketing	occasionally
interrupt	length	marriage	offer
invisible	level	married	offered
irrational	levelled	marrying	offering
irregular	leveller	matters	offertory
irreplaceable	liar	mayonnaise	opportunity
irreproachable	librarian	mechanic	optical
irresistible	library	medical	oratorios
irresponsible	licence	medicine	oscillate
irreversible	license	merciful	outrageous
island	lie	metric	overheard
its (possessive)	limitation	millionaire	Pacific
it's (it is)	limited	minded	paid
jockey	lives	mini	paralleled
joyful	loaves	miscarriage	parliament
judgement	locality	misconduct	pattern
judgment	locked	misgivings	peaceable
juicy	logic	mislead	peaceful
jumped	loneliness	misshapen	people
just	long	misspell	perceive
kettle	longer	misspent	perspiration
kicked	love	mistake	perspire
killed	loved	mistakenly	Peru
kimonos	loveless	mnemonic	phlegm
kissed	lovely	mortgage	phlegmatic
kitchen	lover	mosquitoes	photograph
knee	loving	mountaineer	physical
knife	madder	mouthful	pick
knives	madly	muscle	picnic
knot	madness	muscular	picture
know	magic	music	pie
knowledge	maintenance	musical	piece
label	malign	nation	pierce
labelled	malignant	national	pitiful
labelling	manageable	necessary	planned
ladies	managed	neighbour	planner
laid	management	neither	planning

planted	reality	residence	scion
plastic	realize	resignation	scissors
playful	really	retriever	secret
plentiful	rearmament	return	secretary
plough	rearrange	reusable	seize
plumber	recall	revel	select
political	receipt	revellers	selves
poorly	receive	revelry	sensible
potatoes	received	reversal	sentence
practical	recent	reversible	sentimental
practice (noun)	reception	revise	separate
practise (verb)	reconstruct	revision	separately
precede	recorded	rhythm	service
preceding	re-entry	riddance	serviceable
prefer	refer	ridge	servicing
preferable	reference	right	settee
preference	referral	righteous	shared
preferment	referred	rite	sheikh
preferred	referring	robbed	shelved
preferring	refrigerator	roofs	she's
prefix	regret	rough	shield
present	regretful	roughage	shipment
priest	regrettable	sadden	shipping
proceed	regretting	sadder	shriek
proceeding	reign	sadly	sick
progress	rein	sadness	siege
pronounce	reject	safely	sign
pronounceable	relation	safes	signal
pronounced	relative	said	signature
pronouncement	reliable	sandwich	signet
prophecy	relied	satisfying	signet ring
prophesy	relief	sausage	sincerely
protect	relieve	scarcity	sincerity
protein	rely	scarfs	sinful
protest	relying	scarves	single
psychology	remember	scattered	sinner
pterodactyl	remind	scatters	sinning
published	reopen	scenic	skein
quarrel	repayment	scent	skies
quarrelling	repellent	sciatica	skilful
quarrelsome	replying	science	skinful
questionnaire	reprieve	scientific	skinless
Raj	rescue	scientist	skinned
react	reservation	scimitar	skinner
real	reserve	scintillate	skinning

skinny	take	transference	unusual
skipping	taken	tranquillity	used
sleigh	taking	transatlantic	useful
sleight	target	transfer	useless
slimming	targeted	transferable	usual
slimness	targeting	transferred	usually
slipped	tariffs	transferring	vacancy
slipper	tattoos	transform	veil
slippery	technical	transformation	vein
snobbery	technique	transport	vicar
snobbish	temper	travel	volcanoes
sock	temperature	traveller	walked
soft	terrific	travelling	wanted
soften	Thames	trick	was
softer	their (*poss.*)	trough	wasted
solos	there (*place*)	true	Wednesday
solve	thereabouts	truly	weigh
sombreros	thereby	trustworthy	weight
somewhere	thereto	Tuesday	weir
sopranos	they're (*they are*)	turf	weird
sought	thick	turned	we're (*we are*)
spelled	thief	turves	wharfs
spies	thieves	twelve	wharves
spiv	thorough	twentieth	what
spoiled	those	twenty	where
spoonful	though	twice	whipped
spotless	thought	twins	who's (*who is*)
spotty	thoughtful	two (*number*)	whose (*poss.*)
station	tie	umbilical	wider
stationary	to (*direction*)	umbrella	width
stationery	tomato	unaided	wilful
stick	tomatoes	unavailable	wit
studios	tonic	unconscious	witless
studious	too (*also*)	understanding	witness
submission	top	uneasy	witty
substitute	topic	uneven	wives
suburb	topical	unforgettable	wolves
successful	topless	unforgivable	wonderful
supplied	topmost	unhappy	Worcester
supplier	topper	unheard	word
supplies	topping	unheard of	work
sword	tornadoes	unnatural	world
swore	torpedoes	unnecessary	worldly
sworn	tough	unnerving	worm
syllabification	traffic	unpopular	worried

worry	worst	write	you're (*you are*)
worse	worth	yield	zoos
worship	wright	your (*poss.*)	

BOOKLIST

CAREY, G. V. *Mind the stop: brief guide to punctuation* Penguin, 1971.
DAVIDSON, G. W. ed. *Chambers pocket guide to good spelling* Chambers, 1986.
MORRIS, M. *Solve your spelling problems: a new way to learn* Pitman, 1982.
QUILLIAM, S. *Which word?* Nisbet, 1981.
TEMPLE, M. *Pocket guide to spelling* John Murray, 1985.
THOMPSON, D. *Spelling and punctuation* Oxford U.P., 1981.

In addition, there are several spelling dictionaries available. Have a look in bookshops and pick one that suits you best.

You may be interested to know that The Open College offers a 'distance learning' course on writing with or without a tutor to help you. For details write to: The Open College, P.O. Box 35, Abingdon, OX14 3BR. (Tel: 0235 555444)

In addition to books there are software packs available to help you overcome spelling problems. Two that you might find useful are:

Spelling it out: Context (BBC Soft), suitable for all the BBC series of micros. Write for details to BBC Soft, P.O. Box 22, Wellingborough, NN8 2RE.

Spelling (ALBSU), suitable for BBC Model B (1.2 OS). Write for details to: Adult Literacy and Basic Skills Unit (ALBSU), Kingsbourne House, 229–231 High Holborn, London WC1V 7DA.